# Smart Moves That Successful Managers Make

# Smart Moves That Successful Managers Make

✦

## 2nd Edition

*Cassandra Mack*

iUniverse, Inc.
New York Lincoln Shanghai

# Smart Moves That Successful Managers Make
## 2nd Edition

Copyright © 2007 by Cassandra Mack

iUniverse books may be ordered through booksellers or by contacting:

iUniverse
2021 Pine Lake Road, Suite 100
Lincoln, NE 68512
www.iuniverse.com
1-800-Authors (1-800-288-4677)

Because of the dynamic nature of the Internet, any Web addresses or links contained in this book may have changed since publication and may no longer be valid.

The views expressed in this work are solely those of the author and do not necessarily reflect the views of the publisher, and the publisher hereby disclaims any responsibility for them.

ISBN: 978-0-595-46371-8 (pbk)
ISBN: 978-0-595-90664-2 (ebk)

Printed in the United States of America

# Contents

# *Introduction*

Think about the most respected and influential managers whom you know. What makes them so valuable—almost indispensable to their companies and organizations? What makes them so effective and influential?

Outstanding managers possess a combination of skills and characteristics that enable them to lead and manage effectively. Outstanding managers are: highly skilled at building momentum, motivating others, seeing the big picture and coming up with innovative ways to fulfill the company's mission. They're able to work with diverse groups of people. And most importantly, they are adept at handling the challenges and opportunities that come with management. These are just a few of the exciting things you'll learn in *Smart Moves That Successful Managers Make*.

Whether you're a department manager, division head, project manager, team leader or an executive director of a young organization, *Smart Moves That Successful Managers Make* will help you lead and manage more effectively. Throughout this book, you will notice that I use the term manager to refer to the aforementioned job titles. Although each title carries a slightly different job function, in some capacity they all manage people. I also thought it would be cumbersome for you, the reader, if I constantly listed all of the job titles that fall under management. I hope this consideration makes the book an easier read for you.

*Smart Moves That Successful Managers Make* started out as a workshop. In this workshop I teach managers how to avoid the kinds of mistakes that decrease productivity and bring out the worst in their employees. I also teach them how to put a plan in place to manage themselves, their people and their projects. Each time that I conducted this workshop, I learned a lot about what successful managers do and what they don't do. I learned about different management styles at work, the importance of having a manager's pledge, strategic planning skills and why it is vital that managers learn to groom ambassadors instead of simply managing employees.

In my workshops, I lead managers through a series of self-assessment exercises, brainstorming sessions and skill building activities designed to help them: identify organizational and self-imposed barriers to success, nurture their employees' strengths and map out a game plan for growing and advancing in their careers. For example, I encourage managers to develop a personal mission statement as well as a manager's pledge so that they would be better able to make decisions that were in line with their company's vision as well as their core beliefs and values. I challenge managers to treat their employees like partners instead of subordinates so that their employees would have a greater incentive to invest their time, talent and resources into the company.

As I spoke with workshop participants and read through their letters and e-mails, it was clear that the strategies were working, but they had additional questions that went beyond the workshop. They wanted more in-depth information and exercises to support the strategies that I had outlined in the workshop. I began filing their questions and dividing them into categories such as: building morale, handling office politics, becoming more marketable and influential, balancing career with one's personal life, building alliances and improving one's basic management skills. As a result, *Smart Moves That Successful Managers Make* was written.

As you more forward in your professional journey, the most powerful motivating force that will help you put the strategies in this book into practice other than your commitment to excellence, is to partner with other Smart Moves Managers who are committed to excellence. This really is essential, because you will achieve faster and greater results with the support and encouragement of like-minded people. This is what makes the workshop experience so powerful—the sense of community and connection.

Once you find a partner or group of people who have a vested interest in becoming Smart Moves Managers, follow these three guidelines:

1. Touch base weekly to motivate and support one another. Connect in person, over the telephone or by e-mail.

2. Let your partner or partners know what section of the book you want to work on and work on that particular section.

3. Set a date and time to reconnect and discuss your progress, challenges and action plans.

One last thing: *Smart Moves That Successful Managers Make* is not just meant to be read, it is meant to be utilized. To managers who are looking for quick tips on how to get their employees to do everything that they want without question or who are looking for quick-fix solutions, this book will not be relevant.

But for those who are willing to put in the work, you will find this resource extremely helpful.

After you've read this book and have had some success implementing the strategies, please visit the Strategies for Empowered Living Online Community at: **www. strategiesforempoweredliving.com** and share your success story, a helpful resource or a tip that has worked well for you as a manager.

Thank you for choosing *Smart Moves That Successful Managers Make* as your professional development resource. I wish you continued success.

Wishing You Every Good Thing,
Cassandra Mack

# 1

# *The Smart Moves Manager*

During the last few years, I have become aware of a new breed of managers that I refer to as Smart Moves Managers. Smart Moves Managers are take charge individuals who are proactive about their professional growth, strategic about their careers and who are actively seeking ways to raise the bar and bring out the best in their people. To find out whether or not you are a Smart Moves Manager, ask yourself these five questions.

1. Am I a visionary leader?

2. Do I define my work by my mission rather than my job function?

3. Do I contribute to my company and the people I work with in new and exciting ways?

4. Do I manage and lead my staff in ways that enable them to fully utilize their skills and talents?

5. Am I maximizing my potential by taking advantage of every opportunity that is available to me?

If you answered yes to all of these questions, then I would venture to say that you are a Smart Moves Manager. Smart Moves Managers are everywhere. Even in times of rapid change and financial uncertainty, there are many managers who are making genuine contributions to their people and organizations and who are looking not only for success, but for real significance as well.

# THE 7 HABITS OF THE SMART MOVES MANAGER

Smart Moves Managers don't succeed by accident. They succeed because they consistently practice smart habits. Below are the 7 habits of the Smart Moves Manager.

## 1. Leadership

The successful manager understands that he is not just a manager; he is also a leader. While the manager works to carry out the goals of the organization, the leader serves to inspire, motivate, create new goals and fulfill the organization's mission in innovative ways. While a manager has a plan, a leader has a vision.

## 2. Creativity

The successful manager values and promotes creativity. She creates an environment where her employees are able to think out of the box and come up with new and more effective ways to carry out the company's goals and mission.

## 3. Integrity

The successful manager is a person of integrity. He strives to foster an environment of respect, dignity and mutual accountability. He models the characteristics and values that he seeks from his employees.

## 4. Acknowledgment and Appreciation

The successful manager acknowledges and appreciates her staff, colleagues and her boss. She praises others for their good work and isn't afraid to share the credit. She acknowledges the skills and strengths that others bring to the table. She rewards people for their hard work.

## 5. Service

The successful manager is committed to quality service. He constantly examines and evaluates how his team or department delivers its services. He promotes a culture of service where everyone feels respected and valued.

## 6. Growth

The successful manager constantly challenges herself and her people to move to the next level by learning more and doing more. She challenges herself and her people to stretch themselves intellectually and emotionally so that they can continue to grow.

## 7. Community

The successful manager strives to create a sense of community. He understands that it takes a village to carry out a successful program, so he creates an atmosphere where people can get to know and support one another. He understands that there is no room on his team for backbiting and dirty office politics. He simply won't tolerate it.

## MANAGEMENT VS. LEADERSHIP

What's the difference between management and leadership? Leadership is different from management, but it does not replace it. In fact, leadership compliments management. Not every manager has good leadership skills and not every leader has good management skills. The primary functions of management are to plan and organize through staffing and allocating resources, while the primary functions of leadership are to develop a vision of the future and produce change through motivation and inspiration. Management produces plans and orderly results. Leadership produces strategies and action. Management controls the workflow and ensures that objectives are met by pushing people in the right direction. Leadership motivates people by satisfying their needs for achievement, recognition, meaning, contribution, a sense of belonging and the opportunity to live out their personal definition of success.

You are managing when you:

### Plan and Allocate Resources

Planning and allocating resources are the first things that managers do. By setting targets, reviewing your budget, thinking through all of the necessary steps for achieving those targets and allocating resources to the appropriate places, you are able to begin the work of achieving your company's objectives.

## Organize and Staff

When you organize and staff you are creating an infrastructure and a set of jobs to accomplish your objectives. In this capacity you put a system in place and hire qualified people to implement the objectives through the work that they do.

## Delegate

Delegating is an important aspect of management. When you delegate you assign tasks to your employees and provide instructions so that they can carry out the tasks accurately.

## Monitor and Evaluate

As a manager it's important that you devise a system to monitor and evaluate your employees in order to provide them with tools for improvement and ensure successful project implementation.

## Discipline

Disciplining employees is one of the most commonly avoided responsibilities of management, because it means that you will ruffle some feathers and cause some people to dislike you. But, it is a necessary function of management. When you take disciplinary action, what you are doing is addressing problems that, if go unresolved, could lead to decreased productivity and negative workplace behavior.

## Problem Solve

Managers frequently solve problems in order to identify deviations in the system and implement better solutions. As problems with your team or division arise, you will be called upon to reassess situations and put plans in place to help things run more effectively and efficiently.

## Serve As The Liaison Between Your Employees and Upper Management

As a manager you are the liaison between your employees and upper management. You are the link between those who actually perform the work and those who need the work to get done. In your role as a liaison you are a buffer, a negotiator, an advocate and a translator.

You are leading when you:

## Provide People With A Vision

Whenever you provide people with a vision of a preferred future you are leading.

## Motivate and Inspire

Achieving a vision requires motivation and inspiration. As a leader you need to employ a variety of motivational strategies in order to bring your vision into fruition.

## Initiate Change

No one has figured out how to effectively manage change, but you can initiate it. As a leader you can create the spark of hope and encouragement that will inspire people to change.

## Align People With the Company's Mission

Getting people to buy-into and align themselves with the company's mission are functions of leadership. In order to get people to carry out an organization's mission successfully, they must believe in the mission and see themselves as an intricate part of the big picture. This is where the leader steps in.

## Initiate New Courses of Action

When you hear of someone being a leader, you usually find that the individual has led people through a very challenging task. Or, that he/she has initiated a new idea, launched a new project or initiated a new course of action that positively impacted the program and organization.

## Build Morale and Nurturing Potential

Building employee morale and nurturing their potential enables your people to bring their best thinking, ideas and practices to the workplace. This allows employees to do what needs to be done without you having to constantly tell them.

## Contribute to A Culture of Leadership

Leadership ability does not depend on one's job function. It depends on one's ability to inspire action. When you contribute to a culture of leadership, you communicate the message that everyone has leadership capabilities and you nurture leadership in all of your employees.

## WHY YOU MUST HAVE A MANAGER'S PLEDGE

Having a manager's pledge—a formal promise or set of promises as a continual reminder of what you intend to achieve, accomplish and contribute in your role as a manager will keep you focused on the big picture. It will also enable you to clearly communicate what you want and need from your staff. Drafting a manager's pledge is different from goal setting or strategic planning, because it clarifies the reason for the plan. It provides a point of focus. It involves thinking about your fundamental beliefs, life goals, purpose, values, your company's mission and the commitments that you are willing to make as a manager.

To begin, set aside some quiet, uninterrupted time and respond to the following questions.

- What is your definition of a successful manager?

- Do you embody the qualities and characteristics that you noted in your definition?

- What do you see as your primary functions in your role as a manager?

- What are your core beliefs and philosophies about work? About life?

- What are your top ten values? How do you demonstrate your values when you're at work? What about when you're at home?

- As a manager, what drives you? What fuels your passion? As a leader what drives you? What fuels your passion?

- Where do you fit within the grand scheme of things in your company? What value, assets and strengths do you bring to the table that help to promote your company's goals?

- What opportunities do you see in your position as a manager to serve more and initiate positive change?

- Where in your life could it be said that you are the most focused? How could you apply this focus to the other areas of your life where you are less focused?

- If you could teach a brand new manager three things about the benefits and challenges of management, what would you teach and why?

- What commitments are you willing to make to achieve the things you want to achieve as a manager? What commitments do you expect from your employees?

- What three things do you pledge to do as a manager by the end of this year? In six months? Next month? Daily?

The second and perhaps most important aspects that will aid you in the development of your manager's pledge are the formation of a mission and vision statement. A mission statement captures what you intend to do, while a vision statement captures where you want to be. Your vision is your desired future. Your mission involves the work you will do to bring your vision into fruition. Think of your mission as your calling and your vision as a mental picture of what's to come.

As a leader and manager, it is important that you have a clear vision for yourself, your program and your employees. Think about your organization's vision and where and how you fit into the overall scheme of things. Then, respond to the following sentence stems.

- My company's vision is ...

- My vision for myself is ...

- My vision for my unit/department/program is ...

- My vision for my employees or team is …

Once you have a clear sense of vision, it's time to think about your mission. Every company has a mission statement. This statement defines the purpose of the organization and summarizes why the organization was created. A good mission statement is succinct, contains two to three action words, is easily understood and can be recited in 30 seconds or less.

A smart moves manager not only has a clear understanding of her organization's mission, but also has her own sense of personal mission. She makes sure that any company she works for is in alignment with her personal mission. Review your company's mission statement and respond to the following sentence stems.

- My company's mission is to …

- My mission for work and life is to …

- I believe that my company's mission and my personal life mission compliment one another because …

- I can contribute to my company's mission best by …

Now that you've had an opportunity to think about your vision and mission, it is time to start working on your manager's pledge. Following are two examples of manager's pledges from participants who have attended my management seminars. You can use them as a guide.

### A 32 year old manager working in a health care facility wrote:

*I pledge to be fulfilled and challenged by my work. I pledge to develop a staff who will treat all clients with dignity and respect. I believe in honesty, integrity, fairness and teamwork. My goal is to provide a high degree of care to our clients. I pledge to lead by example and do all that I can to inspire excellence and creativity in myself and my employees.*

### A 46 year old deputy director of a youth service organization wrote:

*My mission as a deputy director is to create a culture that values diversity, partnerships, community engagement and initiative. I pledge to model the qualities of leadership, integrity, accountability, respect and commitment that I seek from my staff. I pledge to set high standards of excellence and invest in the betterment of myself, my organization and my community.*

Take this time out to begin drafting your manager's pledge. Put your ideas on paper. Use this sentence stem to get the ball rolling. (In my role as_____ I pledge to …)

## *IMPROVING YOUR DAY-TO-DAY MANAGEMENT SKILLS*

Study after study indicates that there is a direct correlation between one's management skills and employee productivity. So if you improve your basic management skills, you are likely to improve productivity. Here are 9 skills that you will need to manage yourself and your people more effectively:

## 1. Time Management Skills

As a manager, you need to make the most of your time so that you can get the work done without feeling like you're running on overload. You must become very guarded about your time and routinely let go or delegate things that don't have to be personally carried out by you. Managing your time effectively, allows you to spend more time: planning, organizing, goal setting and troubleshooting. It also enables you to build in what I call *When-The-Stuff-Hits-The-Fan-Time* in the event you ever have to respond to a difficult situation that your employees are not able to handle. Here are some tips to help you.

• Identify and eliminate self-imposed time wasters

• Sort mail before you go to lunch and separate it into categories such as: correspondence that needs a response by the end of the week, correspondence that can wait, magazines and junk mail. Toss what you don't need.

• When preparing to meet an employee for supervision, write out an agenda. Ask your employee to do the same. Set a start time and an end time.

• Always write out your schedule and check it twice a day.

• Maximize each day by planning in advance how you will spend each hour. Write down what you will do for the day hour by hour.

- Take breaks. Even the best of managers cannot crank out high quality work for hours on end.

- Get organized. Keep your office neat. Having piles of paper work on top of your desk and notes in inconspicuous places makes your life as a manager more frazzled than it has to be.

- Use e-mail to respond to messages. E-mail enables you to get your point across quickly and stay in contact with people regardless of schedules.

- Prioritize. Examine your goals and make some tough choices concerning what's most important to you and why.

- Establish deadlines. When you assign tasks give a specific due date. Instead of saying, "Please have it on my desk next week", say please have it on my desk by 12:45p.m next Thursday.

- Sort your tasks by deadline. Set up a system for sorting tasks that are due by the end of the day, end of the week and end of the month.

- Analyze your behavior. Are you imposing time wasters on yourself by not delegating enough or responding to every employee's request or waiting until the last minute to complete important tasks?

## 2. Strategic Planning Skills

Strategic planning can be a time consuming and difficult process, but all managers need to think and plan strategically so that they can prepare for the future and map out a course to make it happen. Strategic planning enables you to look at things in broad to narrow terms. When designing a strategic plan you need to think about the overall mission, the company's goals, the broad implications and the resources you will need. As you begin to think about your plans in broad terms, a more detailed analysis will follow. Your strategic plan should be long-term, because the purpose of the strategic plan is to shape the future of your department or organization. Here are some important steps in the strategic planning process.

- Define the overall mission of your organization and your department.

- Determine the major components of your plan, and make sure that they are in alignment with your company's mission.

- Determine what resources and information you will need to complete each component of your plan.

- Evaluate costs, quality, responsiveness and practicality in implementing each component of the plan.

- Set objectives and define goals.

- Get others involved in the analysis of the plan

- Develop contingency plans.

- Develop indicators to track progress

- List all actions needed to achieve your plan.

- Identify milestones for longer-range goals.

- Identify potential road blocks.

- Monitor progress.

• Re-evaluate the plan.

## 3. Effective Communication Skills

It's not enough to know how to do your job as a manager; you also need good communication skills, both verbal and written. As a manager you need to communicate your vision, objectives and expectations clearly and succinctly. One of the number one problems in just about every organization is communication breakdowns. Here are some tips to help you become a more effective communicator.

• State your expectations clearly and succinctly.

• To be sure that your employees understood your message, ask them to repeat it in their own words.

• Whenever you give directions, ask the employee to walk you through how he/she is going to carry out the task so that you can be sure he understands what you want.

• Don't rush through directions, give your employees enough time to process your message and gain confidence with how you want them to proceed.

• Don't leave too much ambiguity. It is better to give too much information than not enough.

• After giving a deadline, ask employees to provide you with a timetable of when they'll start gathering the data, begin the writing and putting together the final draft.

• Don't disappear after you delegate a task, stick around to provide additional instructions and feedback in case it's needed.

- When meeting with staff, give them your full attention. Don't hold two conversations at the same time it's rude and belittling.

- Pay attention to the other person's response to your message. If you get the sense that the person did not understand you or is resistant to your message, try to find out what the barrier is and address it.

- Use "I" language when communicating information that the other person is likely to have a difficult time hearing.

- Encourage open communication. Create an environment where employees can speak freely.

- Ask for your employees for their opinions and suggestions.

- Speak in plain English. Don't make employees feel like they need a thesaurus to communicate with you.

- Don't preach, patronize or talk down to other people.

- Listen to other people without interrupting them.

- Learn to read body language.

- When communicating in writing; be clear, brief and polite.

- Before submitting any correspondence check for spelling and grammatical errors and read it aloud to make sure it reads the way you intended it to read.

- Keep examples of business correspondence to use as a guide.

- Keep it simple, you're not writing to win the Pulitzer Prize.

## 4. Counseling Skills

Sometimes an employee's personal problems can interfere with their work performance. When this happens, you need to put your counseling hat on. While it is not your role or responsibility to provide counseling in the clinical sense of the word, it is your duty to ask probing questions and address problems that can get in the way of an employee's job performance. Here are some tips to help you.

• Find out what's really going on. Get the facts. Don't buy into rumors or other people's take on the situation. Find out for yourself.

• Focus on how the individual's behavior has affected his performance or negatively impacted the workplace.

• Have clear objectives and communicate these objectives to the employee.

• Ensure privacy.

• Allow ample time for the meeting. Allow ample time for the individual to process what you say. Give them time to respond. Set aside 30 to 45 minutes.

• Describe the problem in detail. Give specific examples.

• Let the employee take responsibility for solving the problem, but give him a definite time frame. For example you could say: *In light of what we've discussed, what can I expect from you moving forward.*

• Summarize your discussion and plan for your next steps.

## 5. Problem Solving Skills

As a smart moves manager you need to be able to solve problems effectively. You need to be able to look at a problem from a multitude of perspectives in order to come up with a workable solution. Here are some tips to help you.

• Identify the primary problem. Although you may be dealing with a number of problems, try to figure out what the major presenting problem is.

• If there are a number of problems, break them down into smaller more manageable parts.

• Try to get to the root cause of the problem.

• Get input from others and implement the best ideas.

• Decide on a plan of action.

• Implement your plan of action.

• Monitor and re-evaluate.

## 6. Documentation and Reporting Skills

Documentation and reporting skills are essential as you move up the company ladder. You need to be able to document and report clearly and succinctly. Here are some tips to help you.

• Write what you need to stay in as few words as possible.

• Be clear about the objectives of your document. Is it to propose a new program, summarize a staff meeting or to have a formal record of a disciplinary measure that you need to carry out?

- Know what your reader expects. Writing a letter to your boss or your board has a different tone than a letter that you write to your clients and customers.

- Keep it short and simple. Spell out what needs to be spelled out. Leave out what needs to be left out.

- Check for spelling and grammar.

- If you are responding to a request for proposal make sure that you've answered all of the questions thoroughly.

- Gather appropriate data.

- Use statistics to reinforce your statements.

- Keep examples of your organization's reports, funded proposals and any other documentation to serve as a guide.

## 7. Project Management Skills

As a manager you need to make sure that projects are finished on time and on budget. If you plan out your steps in advance, chances are your projects will run smoothly. Here are some tips to help you.

- Before you actually take on a project, find out the scope and parameters of the project. Find out exactly what needs to be done, how much needs to be done by you and when it needs to be done by.

- Talk to those around you who are good taskmasters.

- Use a flowchart to visually map out the steps that you will need to take to start the project and bring it to completion.

- Recruit people to help you implement the project. Then, delegate tasks.

- Anticipate potential roadblocks and come up with a plan for dealing with them.

- Keep all team members informed of the project's progress.

- Stay within your budget and time frame.

## 8. Presentation and Group Facilitation Skills

Whether you're presenting a new idea to your board or spearheading a committee meeting, presentation and group facilitation skills are necessary. Presentation skills enable you to sell your ideas and present information clearly. Group facilitation skills enable you to create an environment where honest dialogue and sharing can take place. Here are some tips to help you become a more effective presenter and group facilitator.

- Find out about your audience in advance.

- Tailor your presentation to your audience.

- Plan your agenda in advance.

- Use visual aids such as: flipcharts, overheads, computer graphics.

- Provide a handout that summarizes your key points.

- Get the audience involved. Ask questions. Solicit feedback.

- State the purpose of the meeting or presentation and go over the agenda as soon as everyone is seated.

- When facilitating meetings lead the group through the agenda item by item.

- Help your group stick to the agenda.

- Establish ground rules if the meeting is going to focus on a hot button issue.

- Ensure that everyone has an opportunity to speak.

- Use icebreakers to set the tone for the meeting.

- Start and end on time.

## 9. Goal Setting Skills

Goals are like roadmaps because they help you get from where you are to where you want to go. Managers who have solid goal setting skills are better able to provide a clear sense of direction for their people. You will accelerate your career and increase your effectiveness as a manager by setting daily, weekly, monthly and even yearly goals. Here are some tips to help you.

- Review your company's mission statement and keep your goals in line with your company's mission.

- Meet with your employees and let them know what your goals are: for the department and for each employee.

- Set S.M.A.R.T. goals. S.M.A.R.T. goals are goals that are small, measurable, achievable, realistic and time driven.

- Develop action plans around your goals.

- If goals are extremely broad, break them down into bite-sized goals.

- Display your goals where all of your employees can look at them regularly.

- Consider the obstacles both personal and organizational. Develop a plan for addressing these obstacles.

- Prioritize. Decide which tasks must be done first and which ones can wait.

- List everything that you will need to achieve your goals. People? Resources? Equipment? Training?

- Each time you complete a goal do something to celebrate your success.

## *Don't Just Manage Employees, Groom Ambassadors*

Smart Move Managers consistently let their employees know how valuable they are. Smart Moves Managers don't just manage employees. They groom ambassadors. They treat every employee as a high-ranking company representative. They also prepare their employees for this important role. Managers who groom ambassadors treat employees like partners. They share the power and trust their employees to represent the company in a positive manner. When you groom ambassadors, you set the stage for employees to take a sincere and vested interest in the company's success. You also build loyalty. Following are seven things that you can do to groom ambassadors.

## 1. Give Employees A Vision of Something Larger than Themselves.

Study after study shows that people will work longer and harder when they understand how their individual roles contribute to the bigger picture. When employees know how important their individual contributions are to the larger scheme of things, it gives them a deeper sense of purpose. Here are some questions to consider: How do you help your employees understand how their individual contributions, add value to the organization? Do you make employees aware of the higher purpose of their job functions? If your employees were asked "Why is your job important?" What do you think they would say?

## 2. Be Open to Your Employees and Their Ideas

Managers who groom ambassadors continually ask their employees to share their thoughts and ideas. They encourage their people to speak up, make suggestions and come up with new ideas. In order for employees to feel like they are valued, they need to be able to contribute in a meaningful way. When you create an environment where real sharing and co-creation can take place, employees will give you the best that they have to offer. How often do you encourage your employees to share their ideas? When was the last time you implemented an employee's idea? Are you able to share the spotlight? What about the credit?

## 3. Show Your Employees That You Believe In Them

Nothing makes employees feel more valued than having a manager who believes in them. As a manager one of your primary tasks is to delegate. In order to delegate effectively, you have to believe that your employees are capable of carrying out the tasks. Your employees may not have mastered all of the skills yet. They may not have impressive credentials. But that does not mean that they cannot do the job. You must provide your employees with opportunities to grow into their roles. People tend to do their best work when they have someone who believes in them. What can you do to recognize the potential in your staff, when they have not fully grown into their roles? Are there any employees who you've written off as incompetent who just need a little more pruning? How can you show your employees that you believe in them?

## 4. Foster Initiative, Independence and Accountability

Giving employees room to take the initiative fosters a co-creative environment. There's nothing that pumps up an employee's productivity more quickly than working in an environment where he feels trusted and empowered to demonstrate his personal initiative. Don't just talk about the importance of personal initiative; give employees real independence. How can you foster a greater sense of initiative, independence and accountability among your staff? Do your employees believe that you trust them? Do you trust your employees? If not, what needs to happen for you to trust your employees?

## 5. Share the Power

Successful managers are comfortable sharing power. When you give employees authority to make decisions that not only affect them, but also impact the organization, they're more likely to take greater ownership of their roles. A smart moves manager not only gives her staff authority, but provides them with clear instructions on how to use the authority. Sharing of power requires a tremendous amount of trust, but if you provide your people with clear instructions on how to handle the authority, more often than not, they will rise to the occasion. How much power do you give your employees? What instructions do you provide so that, your employees know how to handle authority?

### 6. View Your Employees As Resources

When you view your employees as resources, rather than people to be managed an internal shift in your thought process occurs. You begin to see your employees as valuable assets. As a result, you look for greater opportunities to utilize them. You ask for their advice. You implement their ideas. You value their contributions. You believe in their work. Do you view your employees as resources? What actions do you need to take in order to demonstrate to your people that you view them as resources?

### 7. Set the Example

As a manager everything you do and say communicates a message to your employees. This is why it's so important that you set the example. If you hand in sloppy work, but demand excellence you will create a culture of resentment. You must be the type of employee that you seek. If you want employees to take great pride in their work, start by taking pride in yours. Be an example of excellence and integrity. What kind of example are you setting for your employees? Do your practice what you teach?

# SUMMARY POINTS FOR CHAPTER 1

- As a Smart Moves Manager it's important to consistently practice the principles of leadership, creativity, integrity, service, acknowledgement, growth and community.

- Differentiate between management and leadership. You are managing when you: plan and allocate resources, organize and staff programs, delegate, monitor and evaluate, discipline, problem solve and serve as a liaison. You are leading when you: provide people with a vision, motivate and inspire, initiate change, align people with the organization's mission, build morale and contribute to a culture of leadership.

- Develop a manager's pledge. Stay focused on the big picture.

- The 9 essential skills that you will probably use daily are: time management skills, strategic planning skills, communication skills, counseling skills, problem solving skills, documentation and reporting skills, project management skills, presentation skills and goal setting skills.

- Groom ambassadors by: giving employees a vision of something larger than themselves, being open to their ideas, showing them that you believe in them, sharing the power, viewing your employees as resources and setting the example.

# 2

# *Twelve Fatal Mistakes Well-Meaning Managers Make*

While most managers have the best intentions and would never knowingly do anything to decrease productivity and bring out the worst in their employees, sometimes without realizing it they do. As a Smart Moves Manager, you need to avoid the kinds of fatal mistakes that could cost you in productivity or credibility. Following are twelve common mistakes that well-meaning managers make. Read them. Review them. Avoid them.

## MISTAKE #1. MANAGING WITH A TIGHT GRIP

As difficult as this may be to accept: *You cannot do it all.* Your success as a manager depends to a large extent, on the contributions of your employees. If you believe that you can do everything yourself, you are sadly mistaken. The more autonomy and responsibility you give your staff, the more you provide them with opportunities to sharpen their skills and grow. The more your staff grows, the more productive and valuable they will become to you and your company. Sounds like a win/win situation, right?

You're probably thinking: I can't even trust my employees with the copy machine, let alone trust them to carry out their job functions without monitoring them closely. Perhaps to some degree this might be true, but if you do not give your staff room to breathe, they'll never make any real headway on their own. And the simple truth is if you do not trust your staff to get the job done and act in the best interest of your organization, then you shouldn't have hired them.

No matter how much power and authority you have, you will not be able to personally oversee every task down to the last detail, nor will you be able to make every decision. It is impossible, because you are only one person. This is why it is important that you figure out what needs to happen for you to gain a greater sense of comfort with your employees. And once your comfort level is increased, you need to pull back and share the power. This is how you build loyalty and inspire initiative. The simple truth is if you treat your staff like they are incompetent, they will act like they are incompetent and they'll resent you. Let's look at some simple ways that you can loosen up your grip.

- Review your to-do-list for the day and turn over one small task to an employee

- Give your staff clear directions. Then, ask them to verbally walk you through the steps that they will take to carry out the task.

- For new or less experienced employees monitor them closely at first, then back up and provide appropriate feedback as needed.

- Meet daily with your key people. Let them know what's expected of them. Then, leave them alone to do their work.

- Allow your staff to improvise. Even if their methods are different from yours.

- When you feel tempted to personally do a job that should be delegated, coach an employee through the task instead of performing the task yourself.

- Resist the urge to interfere or hover over an employee's back to see if they are completing the task to your specifications. Give them the opportunity to complete the task on their own.

- Don't finish what your employees start. If they mess up, teach them how to correct their own mistakes.

- Determine what needs to occur for you to develop a greater level of confidence in your employees' capabilities. Additional training? An attitude adjustment? Improved work habits? A re-shift in thinking on your end? Something else?

## MISTAKE #2. BEHAVING LIKE A KNOW-IT-ALL

The most successful managers know that they do not have all the answers. In fact, they often hire employees who possess skills and knowledge that they don't have in order to carry out their goals. And once they get a sense of their employees' special expertise and strengths, they match the work assignments to each employee's area of specialty. This is how teamwork begins.

As a manager you need to keep in mind that you are one of many sources of information that your employees can look to. But your employees will also acquire knowledge through the professional associations that they're involved in, the books and journals that they read, professional development workshops, their colleagues, previous work experience, and trial and error. This doesn't mean that you shouldn't teach your employees the fundamental skills for your specific industry. It means that once you do, you should back up and allow your people to learn from other sources like: teaming up with co-workers, allowing a more experienced worker to show a new hire the ropes, giving them articles or recommending books that they can read, providing them with company reports, and newsletters, or sending them to a workshop and having them present what they learned at a staff meeting.

Believe it or not, your employees can teach you and help you grow as a manager. Since they are working on the front lines, they often have a better sense of your clients' wants, needs and concerns. And you can use this information to enhance the programs and services that your organization provides. Your job as a manager is not to know everything. It is to develop the people and resources that can fill in the missing pieces. The worst thing that you can do as a manager, is to come across like a know-it-all, because this kind of attitude sets you up to pretend that you know more than you really do. What's worse, your employees will tire of your pontificating and they'll begin to question your competence and credibility.

# MISTAKE #3. FAILING TO PUT A CONTINGENCY PLAN IN PLACE

A contingency plan is a plan that answers the question, "What If?" Unfortunately, many managers don't talk or think about the "what ifs", until they actually occur. By then, it's a little late in the game. Not having a contingency plan in place causes projects and programs to go awry, because life is unpredictable and unanticipated changes are bound to occur. People call in sick; they resign without notice and they also totally botch up projects and plans. Employees don't always follow-thru on assignments. Sometimes they engage in behaviors that could place the organization in a compromising situation. The truth is "stuff happens." And if and when the stuff hits the fan, you need to be prepared. See if the following examples sound familiar:

- Three employees called in sick and we can't find anyone to cover for them.

- The audit is tomorrow and ten of the case records are incomplete.

- A funder wants to visit the program today, to decide whether or not he will continue to fund the program.

- A high profile board member wants an update today on the new project that your company has just launched. Your executive director is vacationing in the Bahamas.

- You're scheduled to leave for your staff retreat in one hour and the consultant who you hired had a family emergency and will not be able to facilitate the retreat.

Do any of these situations sound familiar? If the answer is yes, then wouldn't a contingency plan make sense? While a contingency plan won't prevent life's, "what ifs," from occurring, it will certainly help you better prepare for and deal with them.

In a nutshell, a contingency plan is made up of several if/then statements that list the possible ways that you might respond if certain situations occur. Keep in mind that coming up with a variety of if/then statements and possible solutions requires everyone putting their heads together to ponder about different situations that are likely to occur. It's a good idea to develop if/then statements for situations that you believe are very likely to occur and that will cause a lot of damage if they occur.

Begin developing your contingency plan by coming up with a series of "if/then" statements designed to get you to start thinking about how you might handle potentially challenging situations that could occur on the job.

**Example**: *If our training budget gets cut, then we will bring trainers to our organization, instead of paying to send our employees out to training thus saving the organization money.*

Once you've developed your contingency plan, keep your employees abreast of it. Periodically review the plan and continually solicit input from your boss, employees and colleagues. With a contingency plan in place, you can minimize the damaging effects that potentially problematic situations will have on your employees, your program and the organization.

# MISTAKE #4. HIRING THE WRONG PERSON FOR THE JOB

Hiring the wrong person for the job is a costly mistake that a smart moves manager cannot afford to make. It diminishes productivity and it can cost the organization in terms of disciplinary action, extra time spent having to closely monitor poorly skilled and unprepared employees or time lost having to constantly fire and hire people.

The four most common reasons that managers hire the wrong people are: they are not clear about the kind of person they want for the job, they do not analyze the job in its entirety, they do not screen applicants thoroughly enough and they do not utilize the probationary period effectively.

### • *Not Being Clear About the Kind of Person You Want for the Job.*

Just like you need to get a clear picture in your mind of how you want your program, department or division to run, you also need to get a mental picture of your preferred employee. What type of person do you want working for you? What skills, attributes and strengths will he/she posses? How and where will he/she fit into the mission of your program and overall organization? The answers to these questions will help you in developing a clear picture of the kind of person you want for the job.

### • *Not Analyzing the Job In Its' Entirety*

Most of the time a job appears one way on paper, but comes with a lot more responsibility and challenges once it is carried out. To hire the best person for the position, you need to think through all of the little details that come with the job and make sure that the prospective employee is up for the challenge. Is the person expected to work late and come in on weekends? Are there other duties that are not indicated in the employment ad, but still need to be carried out? Are there travel requirements? Will the individual be required to be available by pager or cell phone outside of their normal work schedule? Are there any physical or emotional challenges that the candidate needs to be able to handle?

### • *Not Screening Applicants Thoroughly Enough*

No one with an ounce of common sense is going to openly come out and say, "I've doctored up my resume to get in the door." It is your responsibility as a manager to screen applicants thoroughly. Ask applicants to provide references from former bosses, colleagues and even their former employees if they are applying for a management position. Always follow-up on references and ask open-ended questions that will provide you with detailed information about the applicant. During the interview provide examples of challenging situations that the candidate might face and ask about how they might handle these situations. Ask for copies of degrees, certifications and any awards that are listed on an applicant's resume especially, if you intend to grant a second interview. Ask for a writing sample if the applicant is expected to do extensive writing. The bottom line is you need to find out as much as you can about an applicant in order to ensure that you are choosing the best person for the job.

### • *Not Utilizing the Probationary Period Effectively*

In every situation there are going to be winners and there are going to be losers. The workplace is no different. Sometimes an individual will have an impressive resume, ace the interview and thoroughly convince you that he/she is the best candidate for the job. Then when it's time to show and prove, they don't deliver, or you find out that you have a complete and utter nut on your hands. Sometimes no matter how carefully you check and screen your applicants a couple of doozies will slip through. That's the beauty of the probationary period. It provides you with an opportunity to figure out if the person you initially hired is right for the job. It also allows the employee to figure out if the job is right for him. This is the time that you need to: figure out if the individual can adequately handle all of the challenges and responsibilities that come with the position, pay attention to time and attendance patterns, get a solid handle on how the individual gets along with co-workers, and pay attention to attitudes and behaviors that are not in alignment with the company's culture, image or mission.

## MISTAKE #5. TRYING TO DO EVERYTHING YOURSELF

Most managers know that it's wise to delegate, but some just can't seem to resist the inclination to try to do everything themselves. The more you delegate task-related work like: data collection, program documentation, meetings that focus solely on front-line issues; the more you'll be able to focus your attention on process-related work like: planning, coaching, problem-solving, mentoring, goal-setting, employee motivation and retention as well as thinking about ways to add more value to your organization.

One of the leading causes of stress for managers is the inability and unwillingness to delegate. Poor delegation skills lead to poor time management and poor time management leads to unnecessary stress and burn out. It's important for managers to accept that they cannot be everywhere, do everything and make every decision. Utilize your time and energy more effectively by delegating. Here are some tips to help you delegate more effectively.

- Communicate what you need your employees to do in a clear and concise manner.

- Make sure that your employees understand what you want and need from them.

- Ask for feedback to ensure that the tasks you've assigned will be carried out correctly.

- Start with small tasks first and as your comfort level increases assign greater tasks.

- Set a date that the task needs to be completed by.

- Ask the employee if he/she foresees any problems with carrying out the assignment and help them resolve the problem.

- Let the other people in your department know that you've given your designated person full authority to move forward with the assignment or project.

# MISTAKE #6. BEHAVING LIKE DR. JECKYL AND MR./MS. HYDE

A major source of stress for many employees is dealing with a moody and inconsistent manager. They never know how their day is going to end up, because the quality of their workday usually depends on what side of the bed their manager woke up on. So they go to work day in and day out feeling like they have to walk on eggshells in order to avoid ending up on the manager's hit list. Not only does this kind of inconsistent and immature behavior negatively impact on employee morale and productivity, it's completely nuts.

Your employees are not paid to deal with your moods; they are paid to work. You'll kill off any and all incentive and enthusiasm if you are unable or unwilling to keep your moods in check. Here are some tips for becoming more consistent.

- If you're having a bad day, don't take it out on your employees. It's not their problem.

- Keep your word. Do what you said you were going to do.

- Don't play favorites. It breeds resentment.

- If you think you might be tempted to waiver back and forth on an issue, give yourself time to fully process the issue before making a decision that you cannot follow thru on.

- If you have difficulty keeping your moods under control, do the necessary self-work to find the root cause of your mood swings and make a commitment not to be ruled by your moods.

# MISTAKE #7. FOCUSING ON PERSONALITY RATHER THAN WORK PERFORMANCE.

If you've been in management long enough then you already know that you'll have employees who you'll like and employees who will constantly agitate you and work your last nerve. And while you may want to occasionally strangle a hard-to-take employee, in order to be a fair and impartial manager it's important that you judge employees based on their work performance and not on your personal preference. When you focus on personality rather than work performance, you'll be more inclined to nitpick and allow small annoyances to impact your professional judgment. And if you do this, other employees will notice and they will begin to question your professionalism and competency in dealing with different personality types. They may smile in your face and dance to your beat in public, but they won't respect or believe in you. And this is no way to run your division.

Let's say that you are managing an employee who is a season veteran with your company and comes across like a know-it-all. Whenever you assign her a task she almost always suggests a better way of accomplishing the task and her style of working conflicts with your style. What do you do? Do you write her off as a difficult employee, deal with her at arms length and look for ways to get her out of your department? Or, do you try to partner with her, build on her strengths, tell her what you want and need and utilize her to mentor new hires? You'd be surprised how much more you can accomplish if you focus on work performance rather than personality.

# MISTAKE #8. NOT MAKING EMPLOYEES FEEL VALUED AND APPRECIATED.

Everyone needs to feel valued and appreciated. Although you may think that it's not your job to make your staff feel appreciated, if you want them to work at their full potential, then you need to make morale one of you key priorities. It's difficult to give a job your all and go above and beyond the call of duty if you are never acknowledged for your good work. Yet many managers believe that it's not their responsibility to motivate their employees. But the truth is you have a tremendous impact on how your employees feel about their work. The better your employees feel about their work, the better they will perform.

Think about a tough day that you've had recently—maybe you didn't get funding for the new program you proposed, or an auditor was extremely critical of your department. Just when it seemed like your day was going to end on a sour note, your manager comes by to tell you what a wonderful job you did on the presentation you made last week. While your manager's favorable comments may not make you forget about all your troubles, they certainly boost your morale. This is what you need to do for your employees.

Here are some simple ways to show your employees that you appreciate and value them.

- Personally congratulate your employees when they do a good job.

- Write a detailed thank you letter describing what you're most pleased with and why

- During a staff meeting, publicly acknowledge an employee who does an outstanding job.

- Have a pizza party or an elaborate breakfast to celebrate your team's accomplishments.

- Ask your CEO or Executive Director to call an employee personally to thank him for a job well done.

- Write an article about an outstanding employee for your company newsletter.

- If you successfully passed an audit or a team project went particularly well, let your staff take the rest of the day off with pay, give them $10 gift certificates to Starbucks, Barnes & Nobles or Tower Records, or arrange a catered lunch for employees and their spouses.

- Host a fabulous soiree at your house.

## MISTAKE #9. ALLOWING CONFLICTS TO GET OUT OF HAND BEFORE YOU ADDRESS THEM

Conflict is stressful. If left unresolved, it can lead to a tense work environment. While you don't want to referee every little disagreement, you certainly don't want to let conflicts get out of hand before you step in. If a problem is affecting the employees ability to function appropriately and they are either unwilling or unable to resolve it themselves, then you must address it. An unresolved conflict operates much like poison, if you allow a small amount into your system; it eventually eats away at the entire body. Conflict is a natural consequence of working with others. It can even be healthy if it enables employees to come up with different ways to enhance services, but when it stems from one employee's dislike for another or the inability to get along with others, it can be damaging. Here are some guidelines for dealing with conflicts.

- Encourage the employees to work it out on their own. Then, have them get back to you with their resolution. If the conflict has been handled successfully, congratulate them for their efforts and move on.

- If employees cannot resolve the problem on their own set up a meeting and mediate the conflict.

- Establish time driven goals for each employee and state what will happen if the stated goals are not met within the designated time frame.

- Deal with critical issues first, then move on to less pressing issues.

- Set up a meeting to review progress and if no progress has been made, find out why and try to come to a fair resolution.

- If one or both employees refuses to try to resolve the conflict, follow-thru on your stated consequences.

## MISTAKE #10. FORGETTING TO MANAGE YOUR MANAGER

One of the most common mistakes that managers make is forgetting to manage up. Your ability to satisfy your boss is critical to your success as a manager. Managing up is about knowing what your boss wants and expects from you and being able to deliver it. The best way to find out what your boss wants and needs from you is to simply ask. Some questions that you might want to ask are:

- What do you need to see from me in order for you to feel like I'm performing a satisfactory job in my role as a manager?

- What kind of work and personality style best suits your way of working?

- What do you currently view as my strengths?

- What do you see as my areas for further development?

- In your opinion what would be the most effective way for me to carry out my role?

- What do you see as my primary role as a manager working in this department/division/program?

- Are there other things that you would like to see me doing that currently I am not? Is there anything that you would prefer I do less of?

The answers to these questions should provide you with more information about what your boss wants and needs from you. When you ask these questions tread carefully, especially if you are dealing with a boss who is not accustomed to working with self-directed individuals. Here are some more tips for managing your manager.

- Always keep your boss informed, particularly about problems that he/she may find out about. Most bosses want to look like they have everything under control. So don't make your boss look incompetent.

- Tell your boss what you need from him/her in order to better perform your job function. Present your requests clearly and succinctly. Give your boss a few ideas on how he/she can help you.

- Build your boss's confidence in your ability as a manager. Keep him/her abreast of your accomplishments and successes. If you were able to save the organization money, let your boss know. If you were able to turn around a poorly run department, provide your boss with specific details on how you did it.

- Learn your boss's preferred work style. Adjust your work style to compliment his/hers.

- Make the most of the time you meet with your boss by soliciting constant feedback, reviewing performance goals and plans and keeping him/her abreast of your division's progress.

## MISTAKE #11. NEGLECTING TO INVEST IN TRAINING AND DEVELOPMENT.

Far too many managers believe that once they reach a certain level of success in their careers, they no longer need any training or development. But the truth is that in order to continue to grow, you need to invest in your professional development.

Even if you're the executive director you can still learn something new and you're your organization to the next level.

Further, many managers use the sink or swim approach when it comes to training new employees. They hire a new employee show him to his desk and leave him to find his own way. Then, blame the employee if he doesn't grasp the work quickly enough.

Smart Moves Managers know that providing employees with formalized training pays off for the employee and the organization. The employees have an opportunity to sharpen their skills and the organization gets high-performing employees. Here are some suggestions for investing in training and development.

- Establish performance and development goals for each of your employees and allow them to select and attend training workshops that support these goals

- After an employee attends a training program find out what they learned and how they will apply it to their job

- Have employees present what they learned at a staff meeting

- Create a formalized in-house training program for new hires.

- Make time to attend professional development conferences and workshops. Bring the information that you learned back to your boss, colleagues and employees

- Invest in personal and professional enrichment books, audio learning programs and workshops.

# MISTAKE #12. ALLOWING YOURSELF TO BURNOUT

Recognize when you are operating on overload and give yourself a break. Far too many managers work themselves to a state of exhaustion, then wonder why they have no energy left to enjoy life's simple pleasures like: spending time with friends and family, getting in touch with nature or pursuing their personal interests. Here are a few things that you can do to make sure that you don't allow yourself to burn out.

- Take all of your vacation time. You earned it. Vacations are important, they allow you to relax so that you can recharge.

- Limit the amount of work related calls that you make or take, when you're not working.

- Listen to your body. It knows when you need to take a break.

- Every now and then use your sick time for mental health recuperation.

- Get off of any committees that are draining you.

- Turn your work cell phone off when you are not on company time.

- Get plenty of rest. Even God took one day off to rest and the Creator is certainly busier than you.

# SUMMARY POINTS FOR CHAPTER 2

- Don't micromanage your employees. You can't steer the wheel from the backseat.

- Don't act like a know-it-all. It crushes your employees' initiative.

- Develop a contingency plan. You never know when you might need it.

- Make a commitment to hire the best person for the job. Know what kind of person you want to hire. Analyze the job in its entirety. Screen applicants thoroughly. Use the probationary period wisely.

- Don't try to do everything yourself, delegate.

- Be consistent in your moods and actions.

- Don't focus on an employee's personality. Focus on performance.

- Remember to let your employees know that you value and appreciate them. This motivates them to go above and beyond the call of duty.

- Address conflicts before they get out of hand.

- Don't forget to manage your manager. Learn her preferred work style and find out what she wants and needs from you.

- Invest in training and development. Attend professional seminars and provide training for your employees.

- Don't burn yourself out. Simplify your life. Take vacations. Take mental health days.

# 3

# *Leading, Motivating, and Facilitating Teamwork*

I believe that good leadership is an art. Leaders inspire and motivate their employees to achieve the company's strategic objectives by providing their employees with a sense of mission and a vision of something larger than themselves. Leadership knows no limits. Great leaders inspire positive action wherever they go. Leadership is not about authority. It's about influence.

## <u>7 TRAITS THAT EFFECTIVE LEADERS POSSES</u>

Here are seven traits that effective leaders posses:

### 1. Vision

Leaders are visionary people. No matter what position they hold, they are able to see beyond the present. They see the possibilities where others only see impossibility. They see the extraordinary in ordinary, everyday situations. They see the potential in people, even when their actions point to the contrary.

- What is your vision of the future?

- What extraordinary things do you see in the everyday and ordinary?

- Can you see the potential in people, even when their actions point to the contrary?

- Are there any golden opportunities around you that at first glance may look like a difficult challenge?

## 2. Courage

All leaders have courage. They may not realize it. They may not always act on it. But all leaders have courage. Contrary to popular belief, being courageous does not mean that you have no fear. It means that you do what you have to do, in spite of your fears.

- What makes you courageous?

- Recall a time when you stepped out in faith, even though you were terrified of the outcome?

- Recall a time when you surprised yourself with your boldness and courage?

- If you were five times bolder what new ideas, projects, or programs would you initiate? What would you do differently? What are you waiting for?

## 3. The Ability to Welcome Change

Good leaders are receptive to change. They thrive on it. Because leaders are able to envision a preferred future, they understand that change is part of this process. A leader understands that no matter how good things are, there is always room for growth.

- In what ways do you initiate change?

- Identify five things that you've done that make you an agent of change.

- In what ways do you resist change?

- How has your program or organization benefited from your innovation and ingenuity?

## 4. A Sincere Appreciation for Diversity

A good leader values diversity. In fact she encourages it. She does not look for a carbon copy of herself. She looks for people with different opinions, strengths and skills. Smart Moves Managers know that when diverse groups of people come together, great ideas are exchanged.

- What does diversity mean to you?

- How do you encourage diversity in ideas among your people?

- What opportunities are at your disposal to create a more diverse environment?

- What diversity barriers exist in your company, either individual or organizational? Be highly contemplative and completely honest here.

## 5. The Ability to Develop and Sell Ideas

A good leader has to be able to sell the intangible and get others to buy into what they can't yet see. A leader must believe in what he is selling so strongly that he gets others to make an emotional investment in his vision.

• What do you have to sell?

• How can you get others to see the tangible benefits of buying into your idea?

• What are your plans for dealing with the nay-sayers and critics?

## 6. The Ability To Take the Initiative

Leaders must take the initiative in order to move their ideas into action. Since the primary role of a leader is to produce change, the leader needs to set a course of action for change to occur.

• What new plans do you need to initiate?

• What needs to happen to get the ball rolling?

• Who are the people that can help you move your idea into action? What are you waiting for?

## 7. Passion

Leaders must be passionate about their vision in order to convince others to carry it out with passion and enthusiasm. Not only do leaders have to be passionate, they must also possess the tenacity to see their vision through from beginning to end. If others give up or lose their enthusiasm, the leader must muster up the passion to keep the troops marching.

- What projects and programs are you passionate about?

- How do you communicate your passion and excitement to the people you work with?

- How do you rally up the troops, when it's time to get moving?

- What are your plans for dealing with fading enthusiasm and energy lows?

# *THE 3 LEADERSHIP STYLES*

Every manager has his/her own leadership style. Different leadership styles are necessary for different situations. Your leadership style has to do with the manner in which you provide direction, implement plans and motivate people. There are three styles of leadership. They are: authoritarian, democratic and laissez-faire.

## 1. Authoritarian Leadership

Authoritarian leaders tend to be very task-orientated. They focus on the completion of tasks, accomplishment of objectives and the effectiveness of the employee or team. Authoritarian leaders emphasize deadlines, structure tasks, enforce policies and go to great lengths to ensure that everyone is pulling his/her weight. Under the authoritarian style of leadership employees do not experience the feeling of teamwork, because managers tend to differentiate employees based on their individual contribution to the program.

## *When Authoritarian Leadership Is Effective*

- When time is limited.

- When team members have been given every opportunity to work as a team, but cannot or will not agree on an important decision.

- When employees do not posses the skills and knowledge to get the work done.

## *When Authoritarian Leadership Is Ineffective*

- When trying to foster a sense of team spirit.

- When working with skilled and knowledgeable employees.

- When trying to promote personal initiative and creativity.

## 2. Democratic Leadership

Democratic leaders involve the group members in planning and carrying out the work. They also involve employees in the decision making process. Promotes a sense of teamwork among employees. Tries to make each employee feel valued while still focusing on the bottom line. Involves employees in the diagnosis of their problem areas, contributions and their areas of growth. Democratic leaders treat employees as teammates rather than subordinates. Employee satisfaction and relationship building are primary concerns. Builds an employee's self-confidence through positive feedback and recognition of skills and worth.

### *When Democratic Leadership is Effective*

- When trying to build trust with employees.

- When trying to build an employee's confidence in his skills and capabilities.

- When employees are self-motivated.

### *When Democratic Leadership Is Ineffective*

- When employees are unmotivated.

- When a high degree of conflict exists between employees.

- When an employee is operating from an agenda that is in direct conflict with the goals of the project or program.

### 3. Laissez-Fair Leadership

Laissez-fair leaders provide little or no direction for employees. Allows decisions to be made with little or no input. Does not do much coaching and monitoring, but will assume responsibility when necessary.

### *When Laissez-fair Leadership is Effective*

- When working with highly-skilled employees

- When working with highly-functional, skilled and motivated teams.

- When employees can do the task in their sleep

## *When Laissez-fair leadership is Ineffective*

- When working with new hires, unmotivated employees or low skilled workers

- When working with employees who need to be told what to do and exactly how to do it.

- When there's little or no team cohesiveness.

Which leadership style is most effective? It depends on the situation and the employee or employees. Ideally, a combination of all three would probably produce the best results. To determine which leadership style to will fit best, use, the four-step leadership style determination process: 1.) Examine the situation. 2.) Reflect on the employee's strengths and weaknesses. 3.) Think about what you're trying to accomplish. 4.) Then, implement the leadership style that you believe will be most effective in achieving your goals.

Following are 25 questions designed to give you greater insight into your leadership style.

1. Do you define problems for your employees or do you encourage employees to define their own problems and come up with solutions?

2. Are you more concerned with employee motivation or employee satisfaction?

3. How are decisions made in your department or division?

4. How are conflicts resolved in your department or division?

5. How is the work distributed and carried out in your department or division?

6. How is teamwork promoted in your department or division? Are the team's ideas implemented? Who gets the credit when the team's ideas are implemented?

7. How much authority do your employees have?

8. Do you believe that all good ideas have to come from you?

9. When was the last time you allowed your employees to make a decision that impacted on your department without interference from you or someone you've appointed as your eyes and ears?

10. What percentage of decisions are made by you without any input from your employees?

11. What percentage of decisions are made by your employees without any interference from you?

12. Is your leadership style based on equality or power and authority?

13. Do your employees feel good about themselves when they work with you?

14. Do your employees feel respected and empowered?

15. What is your system for making sure that your employees stay abreast of changes that occur within the organization and issues that impact them?

16. What kind of example are you setting?

17. If your employees were asked to describe your leadership style in detail, what do you think they would say?

18. If someone were to videotape you at work addressing a conflict or problem with an employee what would it reveal about your leadership style?

19. What kind of commitment do you expect from your employees? What kind of commitment have you shown?

20. Can you recall at least three examples of compassionate, yet effective leadership that you have seen in your career? How can you show more compassionate?

21. What are the ways that you inspire and provide direction for your people?

22. What are your strengths as a leader?

23. What are your weaknesses as a leader?

24. How can you use your strengths to improve upon your weaknesses?

25. List one aspect about each of your employees that you are most proud of.

The answers to these questions should provide you with greater insight into your leadership style.

# THE 5 PRE-REQUISITES FOR MOTIVATION

At the core of a high performing workforce is the quality of the relationship that each employee has with his manager. Bringing out the best in your employees is all about how people are treated, inspired and challenged. The type of work environment that a manager creates is an important aspect of building morale and motivating employees.

True and lasting motivation is internal; it comes from within. But as a manager, you can create a climate that fosters motivation if you understand the five pre-requisites for motivation. They are: security, fairness, commitment, respect and opportunities for growth and advancement.

## 1. Security

It will be difficult for your employees to put their best efforts forward if they are constantly made to feel like their jobs are on the line. Employees need some degree of job security in order to thrive in the work place. Managers who use threats and intimidation to keep employees in line greatly hamper their employees' sense of security. Even in times of downsizing and financial uncertainty there are things that managers can do to help employees maintain a sense of personal power and control. Managers can: keep employees abreast of any changes that occur within the organization that could potentially affect them, encourage employees to sharpen their skills and take advantage of every opportunity to build their experience portfolio, create opportunities for employees to develop real connections with one another, encourage staff to take good care of themselves and not introduce too many changes at one time.

## 2. Fairness

Fair treatment is an important criterion for employee motivation. If employees believe that they are not being treated fairly, they will not be motivated to do their best work. As a manager you need to remember that your employees are constantly watching you. They watch what you say, what you do and how you treat others. If an employee believes that you are playing favorites with another employee, resentment will eventually set in. Keep this in mind as you delegate tasks and authority to your staff. While you cannot treat everyone the same, you can treat everyone fairly.

## 3. Commitment

Many employees complain that their managers show little or no commitment. While this may not be the case with you, it's important that your staff see that that you are committed to them as well as the company. As a manager your priorities will often shift to the priorities of your boss. When employees see constant changes in direction or re-shifting of priorities, they may interpret it as lack of commitment and focus on your end. Take the proactive approach by keeping your staff abreast of any changes in priorities with a clear explanation of why the changes are occurring. Further, help employees to manage transitions.

## 4. Respect

Respecting employees is about displaying genuine interest and regard for their ideas and their work. When you truly respect your employees you not only care about the work that they produce, you also care about their overall development. In what ways do you show your staff that you respect their ideas and their work? In what ways do you communicate to your staff that you care about their overall development?

## 5. Opportunities for Growth and Advancement

I believe that all of us regardless of our stature in life have a natural desire to achieve and accomplish things. Good employees want to sharpen their skills and build on their strengths in order to do more and become more. The manager who creates an environment where employees can grow and advance will produce high performing employees who will go above and beyond the call of duty each and every time. If you do not provide opportunities for growth and advancement, your staff will become stagnant. How can you provide opportunities for your staff to grow? How can you redesign the work to create more opportunities for ingenuity and self-direction?

# *STRATEGIES OF MOTIVATION*

There is no single best way in and of itself to motivate employees, because every employee has different needs. However, there are specific strategies of motivation that you can utilize to inspire employees to take the initiative and put their best foot forward.

No one knows for certain why some motivational strategies work while others do not, why one employee is motivated by one particular strategy while another is totally unaffected by that very same strategy. With this in mind, the best way to motivate your people is to employ a variety of motivational strategies until you find the one or ones that work best. Below are the three strategies of motivation.

## 1. Emotional Motivation

Emotional motivation is about making sure employees feel good enough to become motivated to do their best work. All employees have emotional needs. When you identify their emotional needs you will have a foundation for emotional motivation. As you get to know your employees, you'll figure out which of the four basic emotional needs to appeal to in order to effectively utilize the emotional motivation approach.

- *Achievement*—Most people have a need to achieve something. Achievement oriented people want to develop their skills, take on new projects and stretch themselves intellectually and emotionally. They are generally pleased if you introduce them to new tasks that build on and support each other and if you recognize them for their achievements. To make sure that your achievement oriented employees know that you notice their good work you need to praise them frequently. You can do this by writing a handwritten note on a post it, sending an email or placing a silver star on their desk calendar acknowledging their good performance. Instead of just writing a thank you note, explain how their actions helped your department move closer to its goals.

- *Influence and Visibility*—Some people love to be in the limelight. They like to exert influence and increase their positive visibility. This type of employee will volunteer to lead special events and tends to be very opinionated at staff meetings. The best way to motivate this type of employee is to appeal to his/her need for influence and visibility. Develop their leadership abilities by allowing them to lead special projects. Treat them like in-house experts and ask for their input. Instead of just asking them, "How do you feel about the new project?" Ask them to spearhead a focus group on the project.

- *Belonging*—Everyone needs something to belong to. Employees who need to feel a sense of comradeship can be motivated through the use of teamwork. Give them plenty of opportunities to work in pairs or teams. Give them formal and informal opportunities to interact with co-workers. Once a month take a group of employees out to lunch. You can bill it to the organization if you use the time to get their input on how to better meet your organization's goals. Once a week you can order continental breakfast for employees and give them a twenty-minute break to relax, relate and release.

- *Independence*—Some employees prefer to work independently. They want the freedom to try new ideas and make the most out of a job assignment. If you micromanage them, you'll be met with resistance. The best way to motivate employees who seek autonomy is to give them control without giving up control. The key to doing this is to recognize all the ways that you can give control around: how the work is carried out, how decisions are made, how co-workers interact with each other, how the work environment is set up. Allow people to decorate their workspaces. When assigning group tasks, give the group clear instructions on the goals to be accomplished and let them work out the details. Why not let your staff decide what day and time staff meetings should be held? How about asking your staff to come up with a list of training topics for the year and let them find trainers to conduct the trainings? When interviewing a potential employee, why not allow your staff to interview the candidate as well? If you really put your mind to it, I'll bet you can come up with many innovative ways to give your staff more autonomy and independence.

## 2. Informational Motivation

One of your most important tasks as a manager is to provide informational feedback to your employees. What is informational feedback? Informational feedback is clear and concise feedback that focuses on an employee's performance and how his performance impacts the department and organization. Informational feedback helps an employee to see how his or her individual contributions impact on the program or the company's strategic plans and objectives.

Do you usually rely on an annual performance appraisal to provide your employees with feedback? If you do, you're making a big mistake. Employees need ongoing and immediate feedback. One way to give employees ongoing and immediate feedback is to teach them to evaluate their own work as they do it. For example, if there are specific things that you are looking for as an employee completes a task teach him to identify these things and give her a concrete way to track progress. By making sure employees know how to evaluate their own work, they will be able to provide themselves with ongoing, immediate feedback. To ensure that the feedback is as truthful and accurate as possible, you can group employees into work teams and have the teams evaluate each another.

## 3. Motivating Through Commitment-based Leadership

Alexander Hiam author of, "Motivating & Rewarding Employees", describes commitment-based leadership as a practical approach to motivating and managing employees who are already on the motivational path. Commitment based leadership portrays peak performance as being built on a foundation of high commitment and high competence. In essence, when employees are motivated by internal factors, you will see higher and longer lasting levels of commitment. When people enjoy the work that they do, they are more likely to do the work well.

Commitment-based leadership seeks to build an employee's level of commitment based on his or her motivation to perform the work. In order for commitment-based leadership to occur, employees must feel good about the work that they are doing and they must be in an environment that makes them feel valued and appreciated. In order for employees to be committed, they need to constantly be reminded of how their individual work contributes to the entire organization. The more information they have about why they are doing what they are doing and how it contributes to the big picture, the more they will commit to the work.

When employees are eager to contribute, committed to accomplishing the goals, have a solid understanding of how their individual efforts impact the overall company and are recognized for their good work, you will be better able to achieve full performance commitment.

Once you have their commitment, you need to build their competence level. Do your employees have a solid grasp of the technical and social skills that are required to successfully carry out their roles? Do employees have the support and resources that they need in order to perform at their maximum level?

In addition to implementing the strategies of motivation that were just presented, it's important that you find out the answers to these questions in order to make sure that your employees have what they need to succeed.

When you provide your people with the tools they need to succeed everyone benefits. How? Your people will go the extra mile and become higher performing employees. You'll be able to focus your attention on more process-oriented areas. Your organization will achieve its goals. And to top it all off, you will be viewed as a highly effective leader and manager. Sounds like a win/win situation, right?

# *41 WAYS TO BUILD MORALE AND INSPIRE PERSONAL INITIATIVE*

What can managers do to build morale, inspire personal initiative and energize employees? Plenty. For starters, you can: seek to understand the needs of your employees, connect with your employees in a more meaningful way, give your employees opportunities to make a real impact and create an environment that fosters creativity and a sense of community.

Here are 41 ways that you can build morale, inspire personal initiative and energize your employees.

1.  Pull out the red carpet for new hires. Instead of just showing a new hire to his desk and leaving him to figure things out, leave a welcome package on his desk with all the supplies that he will need and a few extras like: a box of candy, a coffee mug and a stress ball. Make sure everyone in your department drops by the office to formally welcome him. Have a staff person give him a 25-minute personal tour.

2.  Provide all of your employees with personalized business cards and post-its.

3.  Be visible and accessible. Let your employees know that you whole-heartedly support them and that you appreciate their hard work.

4.  Provide unusual benefits like a limited account at the local coffee shop, health and nutrition shop or one paid visit per year to a day spa.

5.  To communicate the message that all employees are important, hold a bi-monthly breakfast with the CEO or Executive Director where staff can contribute their ideas. If the organization implements a staff person's idea, send an announcement by email to everyone in the organization or mention it in your company newsletter.

6.  Do away with executive lounges and reserved parking spots. If you want employees to feel like equals, treat them as such.

7.  If one of your employees is hospitalized send a bouquet of flowers at the company's expense. Organize your department into pairs or groups and visit the employee in the hospital.

8.  Have a dinner party or cook out at your house and invite your entire staff.

9.  Invite your employees to a board meeting and provide opportunities for the board to find out what's working and

what needs to be done differently from the people who are working on the front lines.

10. Give your employees a lot of latitude in deciding how their jobs get done.

11. Form a quality assurance committee made up of all levels of employees and allow committee members to make decisions on improving the organization's service delivery goals.

12. Make sure that employees have what they need to do their jobs effectively. Basic office supplies, access to a computer, an email account.

13. Allow employees to work on projects of their own choosing after they have completed the tasks associated with their job functions.

14. Let employees determine for themselves the best time to take their breaks.

15. If an employee is promoted, allow her to interview her replacement.

16. Ask employees what they need from you to do their jobs better.

17. During stressful times such as layoffs and upcoming audits, spend more time working side by side with your employees. Don't hide in your office.

18. If your organization has a large layoff, give employees two to four weeks of access to the company's computers, telephone, copy machines and resources. Provide them with

employment resources like: wanted ads, job banks and employee recruitment websites.

19. If you are thinking about proposing a new idea to your boss, run it by your staff and get their input.

20. Encourage employees to seek mentors. Even if the mentor works in a different department.

21. Provide each employee with a special notebook to record their ideas and suggestions.

22. Create a "Letters to the CEO" section in your company newsletter and encourage the CEO to respond by the next issue.

23. Sponsor a program on stress management, health and nutrition, love and romance or parenting.

24. Give employees 15 minutes to chitchat and have coffee, tea, or juice before they actually start their work.

25. Hold a staff meeting in a park, garden or at the beach.

26. To encourage employees to invest in their training and development, host an in-house college fair or off-set the cost of an adult education course.

27. Provide your employees with subscriptions to professional trade journals. If you cannot afford to provide each employee with their own subscription, then provide a subscription for the department.

28. Ask your staff to create a list of career development opportunities like: taking on new assignments, developing new skills and sitting on committees. Then create a personalized career development plan that encompasses the items on their lists.

29. Provide opportunities for your staff to purchase equipment and supplies for the office, go to a job fair as a recruiter, organize the company Christmas party or picnic, supervise a cost cutting initiative, design a customer service survey for clients, design a training course or represent your organization in a professional association.

30. Let your department come up with their own rules for handling lateness, high absenteeism, employee conduct, missed deadlines and carrying out work related tasks and advocate to build them into your policies and procedures manual.

31. During work hours take your team bowling, roller skating or to an arcade. Discuss your department's plans and goals and come up with interesting ways to carry them out.

32. During meetings assign each of your employees a specific role: time keeper, recorder, summarizer, process monitor and mediator.

33. Review your policies and procedures manual and make sure that it meets the needs of your employees as well as the needs of your organization.

34. If your team is working under a tight deadline, personally serve them breakfast, lunch or an early dinner. While going

around to each of your employees, find out how far along they are in the process and what you can do to help.

35. Have live or silk plants and framed artwork at each employee's workspace.

36. Create an employee lounge complete with a TV, coffee tables, sofas, a CD player with a selection of CD's, fish tank, flavored coffee, tea, cookies and anything else that you think would be appropriate.

37. Create a fitness room complete with free weights, yoga mats or have an employee teach a 30-minute class during the workday.

38. On school holidays allow employees to bring their children to work as long as they are well behaved. Revisit your policies and procedures manual and look for ways to make your organization more family friendly.

39. If there is a death in your organization, hold a 30-minute memorial service commemorating the life and work of the deceased.

40. Start an employee wellness program designed to promote empowered living.

41. Create a weblog where employees can post new ideas, helpful resources and ask for feedback.

# FOSTERING TEAMWORK THAT WORKS

Team building is often seen as the great solution for getting employees to work together for the betterment of the program or organization. Sometimes the organization's efforts work but more often than not they don't. The #1 reason why many organizations fail at their teambuilding efforts is they expect too much, too quickly, of too many people who haven't had the time to get to know each other or the training to learn the attitudes and behaviors that are necessary for effective teamwork to take place. Further, many managers do not create an environment where teamwork can flourish properly.

In this section, we won't deal with the entire company; instead we'll focus on the team or division that you manage. Now let's talk about what we mean by teamwork. Three characteristics make up the definition of teamwork. First, teamwork consists of a group of people in an interdependent entity working towards a common goal. Second, each member of the team accepts individual and group responsibility for the team's performance. Third, members support one another by filling whatever roles need to be filled and sharing responsibilities in order to achieve the overall goal.

Teamwork benefits an organization tremendously. Research indicates that people are much more effective when they work together and have a sense of comradeship than people who work independent of one another doing their own thing.

For teamwork to be effective, three requirements must be met. First, group members have to be mature enough to put their personal agendas aside for the betterment of the team and company. Second, group members need to be able to put personality differences aside in order to meet the team's goals.

Third, the manager must create an environment where team-work can flourish.

### 1. *Group Members Have to Be Mature Enough to Put Personal Agendas Aside*

A good team is able to put their individual agendas aside for the betterment of the team. This means looking for ways to make someone else's ideas work rather than solely pushing one's own. It also means committing one's self fully to the team and its goals. And finally, it means using one's individual skills and knowledge to compliment the skills and knowledge of the entire group.

### 2. *Group Members Need to Put Personality Differences Aside*

A word here about personality differences: Putting personality differences aside does not mean that you should expect your employees to tolerate inappropriate or disrespectful behavior. It simply means that you should communicate to employees that you expect them to try to get along with each other. Some ways to do this are: speak positively about the team and the organization at every available opportunity, maintain a positive attitude regardless of the circumstances and be respectful and empathic to others.

### 3. *The Manager Must Create An Environment Where Teamwork Can Flourish.*

Managers can encourage effective teamwork or stifle it. Many managers stifle effective teamwork without even knowing it. One way that managers stifle teamwork is by micromanaging their employees. When you do not give employees room to think and act independently, they will not be able to develop their leadership and decision making skills or the feeling of comradeship with their co-workers that is necessary for effective teamwork to take place. Another way that managers stifle effective teamwork is by sending in a team spy. A team spy is a person who you either solicit or who volunteers to run back and tell you everything that the team members say and do when they are not under your watchful eye. This kind of behavior causes a divide and conquer dynamic. It breeds resentment and creates an atmosphere of mistrust. It's also a sure fire way to sabotage effective teamwork. How can managers create an atmosphere where teamwork can flourish? By treating your employees as teammates, having clear goals, recognizing their good work and loosening up your grip.

# 10 Teambuilding Tips

## 1. *Seek Diversity In Your Teams*

The most effective teams are made up of diverse groups of people. Show that you value and appreciate diversity by developing teams that are made up of people with diverse ideas and perspectives.

## 2. *Support Your Team*

Begin by recognizing each member of your team as an individual with individual strengths and talents that when combined make up a powerful team. View your team as a resource possessing strengths and capabilities that you can tap to benefit the company.

### 3. *Build Comradeship*

Hold some of your meetings offsite and get the team together for fun activities. Organize a staff picnic or a monthly staff luncheon.

### 4. *Celebrate the Team's Successes*

When goals are achieved celebrate your successes. Have a pizza party or a staff recognition day to show your staff how much you appreciate their hard work.

### 5. *Provide the Team With Clearly-Defined Goals*

Effective teams don't just happen. They must be developed. For teams to function effectively, every team member needs to have a clear role, clear expectations and clear goals. Team members need to know the team's objectives and how their individual contributions will impact the team. Rules and responsibilities need to be spelled out with everyone in agreement that they will work together as an interdependent entity to achieve the team's goals.

### 6. *Make Workspace Conducive to Teamwork*

Arrange the furniture in a way that allows for maximum group sharing. Dedicate more rooms for group meetings.

### 7. *Implement The Team's Suggestions*

If team members come up with a good suggestion that can boost productivity, save money or bring more money in, implement their suggestions and give them the credit.

## 8. *When the Going Gets Rough Let the Team Stick It Out*

Often times when team members can't or won't agree on important issues the manager steps in and makes the decision for the team. This kind of interference hampers the team process. When team members cannot or will not agree, provide them with some key operating principles and send them back to the drawing board.

## 9. *Let the Team Measure Their Progress*

Allow team members to come up with their own evaluation tools to measure their progress. Provide the team with feedback, but let them be fully accountable for their progress.

## 10. Look for Signs That the Team Is Working Together Well

Some of the signs to look for are: enjoyment of the process and the work, a culture of leadership, everyone's ideas are respected and heard even if they're not implemented, group cohesion, a clear sense of purpose, decisions by consensus and the ability to problem solve and address conflicts within the team.

## SUMMARY POINTS FOR CHAPTER 3

- Practice the 7 traits of an effective leader. They are: vision, courage, the ability to welcome change, a sincere appreciation for diversity, the ability to develop and sell ideas, the ability to take the initiative to get the ball rolling and passion.

- Select the leadership style that's best for the situation, the employee and your goals.

- Seek to meet the 5 pre-requisites for motivation.

- Different motivational strategies work for different individuals. When you get to know your employees as individuals, you will know which motivational strategies to employ.

- Help foster a sense of teamwork by creating an environment where teamwork can flourish.

# 4

# *Making Office Politics Work for You*

Like it or not, office politics are a fact of organizational life. Although your work performance may speak for itself, if you do not learn how to make office politics work to your advantage, then you will not be equipped with the necessary information to navigate your way around your company's political maze. Further, you'll be left out of most major decisions. Making office politics work for you is not about being deceptive or manipulative, it's about having a solid understanding of your organization's culture, a clear picture of the formal and informal expectations, avoiding mistakes that can come back to haunt you, knowing how to use the five sources of power to your advantage and building key alliances. You may not be a politician, but if you consider yourself a Smart Moves Manager, then it's a good idea for you to develop strong political and social skills that will enable you to survive and thrive in any organization.

If you think about the type of people who get ahead most often, it's usually those who are highly skilled at managing office politics. Downsizing, reorganization and budget cuts have made it so that more and more people now have to compete for fewer dollars and resources. And your success as a manager often depends on your ability to get and manage your money and your resources. The more you know about navigating the political tightrope, the better able you will be to advance your goals and plans. This chapter will focus on smart moves that you can make in order to make office politics work for you.

## UNDERSTANDING YOUR ORGANIZATION'S CULTURE

Every organization has its own set of values, beliefs and norms. Every organization has its own way of doing things, in essence, its own culture. Sometimes you can get a glimpse of an organization's culture through its' policies and procedures manual, but more often than not, you find out about an organization's culture through its informal rules and practices. The more you know about your organization's culture, the better able you will be able to tailor your work style, professional practices and professional image to fit with the organization's values, image and norms.

You can find out about your company's culture in a number of ways. You can:

- Talk to different people at work, from the receptionist to executive management to get a clearer picture of how things are usually done at your organization.

- Observe the actions and interactions of influential employees and executive management in order to figure out how and why decisions are made.

- Ask more seasoned employees about the organization's beliefs and common practices.

- Look at who gets promoted and who does not. Find out what needs to happen for you to thrive in your organization.

- Find out what the "real" rules are. There are rules that are noted in writing. Then there are common practice rules—rules that are not on the books, but they are just as important if not more so.

Please take a few moments to answer the following questions.

1. *What are the common practice rules and philosophies in your organization?*

2. *How are the common practice rules different from the rules that are outlined in the policies and procedures manual?*

3. *Are the common practice rules different for upper management than they are for middle management or front line staff?*

4. *How do employees learn about the common practice rules in your organization?*

5. *What happens to individuals who do not adhere to the common practice rules?*

Now that you've had an opportunity to think about the formal and informal rules, the next step is to find out who the formal and informal decision makers are. The formal decision makers are those who are able to make decisions by way of their position or job function. The informal decision makers are those who are able to influence the formal decision makers. You need to know who these people are and you need to build strategic alliances with them. Succeeding as a manager is not just about doing a good job; it's also about building relationships with the right people.

## *BUILDING KEY ALLIANCES*

Building key alliances now and in the future is important to your career as a manager. Your personal and professional success depends on other people. You can only go so far alone, because we all need support, encouragement and feedback from others in order to succeed and flourish.

There are many advantages to building key alliances. For starters, you will have a team of people who will work with you to help you reach your goals. Second, you will be exposed to important information and resources that can help you advance your career. Third, you will be better able to advance your organization's strategic goals.

Here are some simple ways that you can build key alliances.

- Identify key people at work and in your professional network who can assist you in meeting your career goals, and who can help establish your reputation as an asset to your organization and your field.

- Cultivate a mentor and ask him/her to show you the ropes and talk to you about what you need to do to increase your value and visibility.

- Always try to make your boss look good. Never put him/her in a situation where he/she could appear incompetent.

- Let your employees and managers know that you appreciate them and their hard work.

- Attend professional association meetings and volunteer for special projects.

- Develop partnerships with people in your organization who appear to be favored by management and periodically ask for their feedback.

- Be polite to everyone, especially the administrative assistants. It could make the difference in how soon your requests get to upper management.

- If you are trying to learn a new skill, ask someone who is highly skilled in that area if you can observe him at his job.

- Make people feel important and be sincere when you do it.

- Try to learn as much as you can about the people you want to build relationships with.

- Offer to pitch in for a colleague who is going through a personal crisis.

- Let the right people know that they can count on you to be competent, dependable and discreet.

- Expand your social base by seeking advice from people who can provide you with information, support and resources.

- Conduct yourself in a manner that is consistent with what upper management wants, expects, and respects.

Please take a few moments to think about some other things that you can do to build key alliances.

# LEVERAGING THE FIVE SOURCES OF POWER TO YOUR ADVANTAGE

Power is the ability to influence others to act or respond in a particular way. Every employee, regardless of his position has power. Everyone has the ability to influence others. Some people are more influential than others, but we all have power. For many people, the word power has a negative connotation. But the truth is, it's not the power that has the potential to be negative, it's the way in which the individual uses it.

Below are some descriptions of the five sources of power. Think about how you might utilize each to your advantage.

## 1. Personal Power

Personal power derives from your charisma, integrity, leadership ability and credibility. With personal power your ability to influence others rests on your ability to get others to like, trust and believe in you. People with a high degree of personal power are often described as charming, charismatic, trustworthy and inspirational.

- Who are the people in your organization with a high degree of personal power? How do others respond to these individuals?

- How can you increase your personal power? What personality traits do you need to develop or enhance?

- How can you get the message across to others that you are likeable, trustworthy, and credible?

- How can you make your personal power work for you?

- How can you utilize your personal power to advance your career objectives?

## 2. Relationship Power

Relationship power comes from your personal and professional network. From bosses to co-workers to employees, the more connections you have, the stronger your relationship power base. Relationship power is not limited to people at the office, it also includes people outside the office who are able to provide resources and information to you and your organization. People with a high degree of relationship power are often described as well connected or in-the-know.

- Who are the people in your organization with a high degree of relationship power? How do others respond to these individuals?

- How can you increase your relationship power? Who do you need to build stronger relationships with? Where can you go to network?

- How can you get the message across to others that you have valuable contacts and that you're in-the-know?

- How can you make your relationship power work for you? How can you utilize your relationship power to advance your career objectives?

## 3. Knowledge Power

Knowledge power is based on the knowledge and special expertise that you have. For example if you are the only one or one of the few in your division, or organization who knows how to re-boot a computer that has crashed or can spice up your organization's marketing materials with a single stroke of the pen then you have knowledge power. People with a high degree of knowledge power are often described as extremely knowledge-able and competent.

- Who are the people in your organization with a high degree of knowledge power? How do others respond to these individuals?

- How can you increase your knowledge power? What skills and information do you need to learn? Where can you go to get the information you need?

- How can you get the message across to others that you are knowledgeable and competent?

- How can you make your knowledge power work for you? How can you utilize your knowledge power to advance your career objectives?

## 4. Task Power

Task power is power that derives from your job function at work. Some work is more vital to an organization's advance-ment and survival than others. For example, the grant writer whose job it is to secure funding for the organization usually has a high degree of task power. People with a high degree of task power are often described as virtually indispensable.

- Who are the people in your organization with a high degree of task power? How do others respond to these individuals?

- How can you increase your task power? What can you do to make yourself more vital to the organization?

- How can you make your task power work for you? How can you utilize your task power to advance your career objectives?

### 5. Position Power

Position power derives from your location on your company's organizational chart. CEO's, Executive Directors, Vice Presidents and top level managers have a high degree of position power, because their position gives them the authority to make senior level decisions. People with position power are able to enforce company policies, hire and fire and give promotions and raises by the way of their position. They have the authority to act on the organization's behalf without needing approval from a higher authority.

- Who are the people in your organization with a high degree of position power? How do others respond to them?

- How can you increase your position power? What do you need to do and learn in order to increase your position power?

- How can you get the message across to others that you can be counted on to make decisions that are in the best interest of the organization?

- How can you make your position power work for you? How can you utilize your position power to advance your career objectives?

When trying to figure out how to increase your level of influence in one of the five power areas, keep in mind that you can use one source of power to achieve a higher degree of power in another area. For example, you can use the knowledge power that you have from the skills and information you've acquired working at your current position to move up the company ladder, thus increasing your position power. Or you can use the relationship power that you have from the contacts and strategic alliances that you've built to take on more visible and valuable projects, thus increasing your task power.

## *CHOOSING YOUR BATTLES WISELY*

Unresolved conflict is stressful. It leads to a tense work environment, nasty workplace antics and it makes your work life more difficult than it has to be. As a smart moves manager, you need to promote an environment of positive interchange. Believe it or not, when you get into a conflict with someone, you and the opposing party are not the only ones who are affected. Your coworkers, friends and employees are often dragged into the conflict because tension impacts the entire work environment. One of the most effective ways that you can prevent a conflict from getting out of hand is to choose your battles wisely. Before responding to an insensitive remark or slight, ask yourself: "Is this really worth it?" If the answer is no, let it go and move on. If the answer is yes then deal with conflict directly, tactfully and timely. Here are some strategies for dealing with conflicts.

- Describe the problem as you see it. Be specific. Focus on behavior not personality. Site recent examples.

- Use "I" language. Instead of saying: "You are so disrespectful, "say: "When you made the comment about _____ I felt disrespected by you when you said…."

- Explain how the problem or behavior is impacting your work performance, the work environment or your ability to work with the individual. Give specific examples. "We are not meeting the organization's objective of _____." "The time spent bickering could be time better spent working on the project."

- Listen to what the other person has to say. Try to get a sense of the other person's point of view, even if you disagree.

- Analyze the situation. Identify possible solutions.

- Review the possible solutions and agree on a solution.

- Come up with an action plan that both parties can agree on and implement it.

- End on a positive note.

By choosing your battles wisely and dealing with conflict directly and respectfully, you'll be better able to avoid the petty kind of behavior that can cause you to lose your cool and your credibility.

## *SUPERVISING DIFFICULT EMPLOYEES*

What do you do when you have to supervise an employee who behaves like a complete and utter jerk? Someone who seems intent on giving you a hard time. Many problems with difficult employees stem from one of three things: different work styles, personality clashes and different work philosophies.

## 1. Different Work Styles

If you think about your own work style, I'll bet that you prefer to work in a particular type of way. If you're the type of person who is very self-directed and prefers little or no interference from your boss, then you may resent your boss asking to work closely with you. On the other hand, if you prefer constant feedback from your boss, then you may feel unsupported if there are few opportunities to consult with and get feedback from your boss.

Believe it or not, your employees struggle with the same issue. Employees who prefer to work alone, may believe that you are being controlling or treating them like they are incompetent if you work too closely with them. And employees who prefer to work in teams or be in constant communication with you, may feel unsupported if they do not have opportunities for sharing and teamwork.

Rather than dwelling on who's right and who's wrong, figure out if an employee can work in his preferred work style and still achieve your objectives. For example, an employee who prefers to work alone can be given a specific task with a completion date. An employee who needs constant supervision or feedback can be teamed up with a more seasoned employee.

## 2. Personality Clashes

Sometimes problems will occur with an employee because of a personality clash. Maybe one of your employees is a morning person who comes in totally energized and ready to take on the world at 8:30a.m., while you don't really get started until you've had your third cup of coffee. Perhaps, you are laid back and introspective and one of your employees is loud and overbearing. You and your employee seem to have the same arguments and the same power struggles and it's driving you crazy. As a manager, it's important that you are able to deal with different kinds of personalities, even those that you prefer not to work with. Rather than focusing on the personality differences, try to focus on the unique strengths that each of your employees brings to the process. For example, let's say you have an employee who has a photographic memory of the organization's policies and procedures manual and recites it at every available opportunity. Rather than solely focusing on the negative aspect of this behavior utilize the employee as a mentor to new hires. Or, put him in charge of a special project like making sure all of your records are up to date for the upcoming audit. By reframing the negative trait and using it to accomplish your strategic objectives, you put your time and energy into productivity instead of personality.

### 3. Different Work Philosophies

Just about every manager has had to supervise employees who treat the job like one big party. They come in late, take several unmerited breaks and constantly goof off on the job. Or, the employee who is so serious and anal retentive that he makes everyone feel like they're in basic training for a highly combative position with the CIA. Different work philosophies can lead to major problems, unless they are managed effectively. Here are some tips to get everyone on the same page.

• Try to get to know each of your direct reports and find out about their values and work philosophies.

- Pulling from your manager's pledge and your organization's mission statement reiterate your core philosophies.

- Hold a staff meeting and ask employees to develop a work philosophy statement for your department or division.

- Have everyone complete their own philosophy statement or statements before your meeting then discuss your collective philosophies. Think about how you might be able to bridge your core philosophies with theirs'.

## *COWORKERS WHO ARE DIFFICULT TO WORK WITH*

Coworkers who are difficult to work with are usually not that way out of malice or spite, more often than not it has to do with their own agenda, alliances they've built or unresolved issues that have nothing to do with you. Coworkers who seem to enjoy stirring up trouble, promoting workplace negativity or creating adversarial situations usually have poor relationship skills and play out the same dynamics in their personal lives. One of the best ways to handle difficult colleagues is to know when to confront their behavior and when to ignore them. There will be times when it's best to ignore their pettiness and there will be times when you will need to confront the behavior in order to nip it in the bud. Here are some suggestions for dealing with difficult colleagues.

- Try to avoid contact with difficult colleagues. Be polite without getting too personal.

- Let the person know that you have no interest in engaging in an adversarial relationship. Your goal is to achieve your program's objectives.

- Try responding to verbal antagonism by agreeing with the person on points where he might be right. Instead of trying to defend you point of view, you could say, "You're right, I do need to listen up sometimes." This approach throws the other person off guard, because he was probably prepared to go into battle with you. There can be no fight, if you refuse to engage in one.

- Forget about winning an argument or getting even, make it clear that your goal is to resolve the issue and move on.

- Let your overriding message be, "I'm not out to undermine or discredit you."

- No matter what your colleague does, try to maintain your composure. It's better to let your colleague rant and rave and be viewed as unstable, than for you to jeopardize your career by engaging in inappropriate behavior that may later come back to haunt you.

## *WORKING WITH A DIFFICULT BOSS*

If you think you have a boss from hell, you are not alone. Dealing with a difficult boss is one of the biggest challenges that employees face. The most effective way to deal with an extremely tough boss is to understand what most bosses are looking for. Although most bosses may not readily admit that they can be demanding, overbearing, controlling and even inappropriate, many know full well that they need help in the people skills department.

Generally, what most bosses are looking for is an employee who: they can trust even if they are not trustworthy, they can rely on even if they are unreliable and who behaves with tact and discretion. In essence, they are looking for an ally. Although they may not say so, this is what they want. So if you want to get along with a difficult boss, demonstrate that you can be counted on. Here are some tips to help you:

- Keep you boss up to date on important developments. Without wasting the boss's time with unnecessary details, keep him/her posted on internal developments that he/she might have missed.

- Know what your boss's primary goals are and talk about them as often as you can.

- When your boss gives you a work directive, restate it in your own words and ask for a due date.

- Be accountable for your actions.

- Don't take anything personally. Develop a thick skin.

- Set appropriate limits and let your boss know what you need to do your job more effectively.

- Step back and allow your boss to make adaptations or revisions on your suggestions.

- If you're dealing with a manipulative boss, don't complain about what you can't do, state what you can realistically do and when you can get it done.

- When behavior gets out of hand, be willing to draw the line. Don't be afraid to stand up for yourself.

- Develop a stress management plan for dealing with your boss.

- Don't worry about who gets the credit—at least initially. Be willing to give up some of the credit in order to accomplish your strategic objectives.

- Give control without giving up control. Let your boss think that he/she is in control while you learn a much as you can and maximize your work experience while planning your next career move.

## *AVOIDING NASTY OFFICE POLITICS*

Nasty office politics are promoted and reinforced when organizations send the message that backbiting, underhandedness and manipulation are the quickest ways to get ahead. But nasty office politics hurts everyone. It forces people to develop a cover-your-back attitude and resort to deceptive and manipulative behavior. Further, it fosters a hostile work environment. To avoid engaging in nasty office politics follow these suggestions:

- Do not gossip about or bad mouth anyone who works in your organization.

- Do not criticize anyone in public, even if he/she deserves it. By criticizing the person in public you drag other people into your conflict. People have a tendency to repeat what they hear and once the rumors start, you will not be able to stop them.

- If you plan to challenge the status quo, do your homework and do it with tact. Many senior level managers strongly believe in the organization's longstanding policies and practices and may view challenging the status quo as a personal attack.

- Don't be a habitual whiner. Nobody likes a chronic complainer. If the job or organization is that bad take the necessary steps to change your situation.

- Don't pass off someone else's work or ideas as your own.

- When dealing with someone who engages in nasty office politics try to keep your distance. If his/her behavior is directed toward you try to resolve the issue. If the person is unwilling to stop, document the incident or incidents and gather your facts so that you can describe the incident in detail. Then, follow your organization's protocol for dealing with this kind of behavior.

- Keep in mind that when you engage in nasty office politics everyone loses.

# SUMMARY POINTS FOR CHAPTER 4

- Understand the culture of your organization. Get a sense of your organization's values, beliefs and norms.

- Build key alliances. Try to get to know key people in your organization from the secretary to the CEO. Stay connected. Don't burn your bridges.

- Learn how to leverage the five sources of power. Use one power source to achieve a higher degree of influence in another power area.

- Choose your battles wisely. Don't let conflicts take you off your path.

- When supervising difficult employees try to get a sense of their work style, personality, and work philosophies and utilize them to achieve your larger objectives.

- When dealing with difficult coworkers try not to take their behavior personally. And if you need to confront them do it with tact.

- When dealing with a difficult boss, try to find out what your boss really wants and needs from you and demonstrate that you can be counted on.

- Avoid engaging in nasty office politics. It undermines your credibility and professionalism.

# 5

## *Managing for Peak Performance*

Managing for peak performance is all about helping employees take the necessary steps to do their best work. It's about helping them: set goals, chart their progress, prioritize, strengthen their skills, become more self-directed, and become proactive about their productivity.

Managing for peak performance also means being empathic and demonstrating a genuine interest in your people. Because, when you are genuinely interested in the well-being and development of your employees, you seek to understand their values, needs, and motivators. And this enables you to manage from a place of strength and partnership. As a result your people will be more inclined to operate at their full potential.

# HELPING EMPLOYEES BUILD ON STRENGTHS AND IMPROVE UPON WEAKNESSES

Every employee brings strengths and weaknesses to the job. Your secretary may possess great organizational skills, but may need some work in the people skills department. You may have a counselor who has great crisis intervention skills, but may need improvement in her documentation and reporting skills. We all bring strengths and weaknesses to the work that we do. As a manager you must help your people build on their strengths and work on their weaknesses. This way they can deliver their best work.

One of the best ways to help employees build on strengths and work on their weaknesses is to have them identify them. On a separate sheet of paper, write down the questions listed on the following page and ask your employees to respond to them.

1. What strengths do you bring to your job, your coworkers, your department? The organization?

2. How can you use your strengths to enrich this department?

3. What are your weaknesses?

4. What actions can you take to improve upon your weaknesses?

5. How does your specific job function fit into the goals of this program? The organization?

6. What distracts you? What keeps you from being your most energetic and enthusiastic self?

7. What difficult things do you need to do in order to do your best work? How can I assist you?

8. What are you trying to do on your own that you need help with or need to let go of all together? How can I assist you?

9. What excites you most about your job? What challenges you the most? What do you dread?

10. List five things that you believe would improve this department and organization.

The answers to these questions will provide you with clues about your employees' strengths, weaknesses, values, priorities and challenges. Use your employees' responses to these questions as a guide for uncovering their strengths and weaknesses.

Sometimes strengths can look like weaknesses, because some traits have negative connotations associated with them like: manipulative, paranoid or pessimistic. But if you reframe your thinking in order to harness the helpful aspects of these traits, you can utilize these traits to fulfill your strategic plans and objectives. For example, think about an employee who is manipulative. When we think of someone who is manipulative, words like deceptive and deceitful come to mind. But at that same token, manipulative people are often highly skilled in utilizing relationships, resources and their charisma to get their needs met. What if this same individual was taught how to use this trait to build strategic collaborations and obtain resources for the company? This would be an instance where a trait that is traditionally thought of as negative could be used for good. Or let's say that you're working with an individual who is pessimistic. He/she almost always sees the worst in every situations. Who better to do your contingency planning? Since he tends to see the worst in things anyway, you can use this trait to have him think through all the things that could possibly go wrong in your division and come up with a plan for dealing with plans that go awry

Below are nine questions designed to help you begin thinking about ways that you can help your employees get the most out of their workday.

1.  Do your employees have access to the supplies, equipment and resources that they need to do their best work? If not, what are you prepared to do about it?

2.  Are you utilizing any staff members in the wrong capacity? Ex. (An employee with excellent leadership skills with little or no opportunities to lead)

3.  Do you send your staff to training seminars and workshops so that they can learn and grow. If not, why not?

4.  Have you created an environment where creativity and personal initiative are encouraged?

5.  What negative traits in your staff members can be used for the good of your program or organization?

6.  What situation do you have in your department or division that you would like to see turned around? How can you get your staff to help you turn the situation around?

7. What do blessings look like at your workplace? Which of your employees have been a blessing to you and how? Are there any blessings cleverly disguised as problems?

8. Describe your ideal employee. What needs to happen to make this ideal more of a reality? Based on your description, are you an ideal employee?

9. What are ten new ways that you can help employees utilize their underutilized skills and develop their underdeveloped talents?

## 25 WAYS TO HELP EMPLOYEES SET GOALS, PRIORITIZE TASKS AND MANAGE TIME

A big part of your success as a manager involves helping employees set goals, prioritize tasks and manage their time. The sooner you put a system in place that helps your staff set goals, prioritize tasks and manage their workflow, the better able you will be to meet your department's aims and objectives. And you'll meet them on time. Here are twenty-five tips to help you get started.

### 1. Match the Goals to the Organization's Mission

We've already discussed the importance of making sure that your goals are in line with your organization's mission, but you also need to make sure that your employees understand the organization's mission and how their goals help to fulfill and enhance it. For example, if your mission states, "We help children and families develop their full potential through educational services." Then, one of your service goals may be to provide tutoring services to a minimum of fifty children. This goal lines you up with the organization's mission.

## 2. Benchmark

Compare your goals to those set by other departments or organizations doing similar work. See what's working and what's not.

## 3. Help Staff Develop Performance Indicators

How will your staff know when they are closer to achieving their goals? How will they know if they get off course? Help staff come up with performance indicators so that together the two of you can measure their progress. You can ask them to choose two to four indicators that cover the critical areas of your department's objectives.

## 4. Display Goals Conspicuously

Display goals in a clearly visible place like the wall or on a desk calendar so that staff can be constantly reminded of the goals in order to remain focused.

## 5. Encourage Staff to Come Up With New and Better Ways to Meet Goals

At staff meetings and during your one-to-one talks encourage staff to come up with new and better ways to meet goals. Review goals regularly and make sure performance is improving. If your goals are unrealistic or outdated, involve your employees in adjusting the goals so that they're more realistic and reflect your current environment.

## 6. Delegate the Right Task to the Right Person

Get to know your employees. Get a clear picture of their strengths and weaknesses and match the tasks to each person's unique skills.

## 7. Provide Your Staff with Clear Time Frames

When you provide your staff with clear time frames, you give them the tools to prioritize. If an employee clearly understands what you want done and when you need it done by, he/she will be able to get the work done in a timely manner.

## 8. Encourage Your Staff to Work On the Most Dreaded Tasks First

Usually we wait until the last minute to start the tasks or projects that we dread. When we do this, we set ourselves up to work in stress mode trying to get everything done in a short amount of time. Find out which aspects of the work employees dislike the most and have them work on these tasks first. This way they won't be operating under such immense pressure to get all of their work done.

## 9. Help Your Staff Stay Focused On What's Important

Some employees have trouble staying focused on the important issues, because they are trying to do too many things at once. To combat this help your staff figure out the most important parts of their work, discuss priorities with your staff regularly, at least once a week. Have them review these goals monthly and weekly, then break them down into bite-sized action steps.

## 10. Talk to Staff About the Importance of Choosing Action Over Feelings

I used to work in a foster care agency, where I had to fill out a lengthy report called a uniformed case record. I didn't particularly enjoy this aspect of the work, but never the less, it had to get done. If I would have given into my feelings, I would have never gotten around to completing this important document. Talk to your staff about the importance of choosing action over feelings. When employees are feeling down, encourage them to take a ten-minute break to collect their thoughts, read something funny, or do something that picks them up. Then encourage them to focus on their work.

## 11. Help Employees Cut Down Interruptions

Most people interrupt each other in a haphazard way. They call or drop by without thinking about what these constant interruptions do to others. Some interruptions are important, but most are not. Help employees cut down on unnecessary interruptions by helping them to understand the difference between what's urgent, what can wait and what's a complete waste of time. By using this method, employees will be able to handle interruptions more efficiently and effectively.

## 12. Encourage Employees to Develop a System for Organizing the Paper that Crosses Their Desks

A systematic approach to handling the paper that comes across your desk is an important part of managing your workday.

Develop a system for sorting your mail. For example, you can divide your paper into four categories: response, information, toss and leisure. Response paper is anything that requires you to respond or do something. Information paper is paper that keeps you informed about your organization and field. The leisure category is for things like magazines, booklets and newsletters. The toss category is anything that isn't worth your time.

## 13. Encourage Employees to Create Uninterrupted Blocks of Quiet Time

Most people accomplish about half of what they should be able to do in a given workday. Quiet time enables employees to totally focus on tasks that require a great deal of concentration like: writing reports, working on projects, planning, organizing, and doing anything else that requires analytical skills and creativity. Employees won't find quiet time, they have to create it and you have to help them do it. For at least ½ hour allow employees to go to a quiet space so that they can analyze and create. Remember, if the goal is to increase productivity, you must give your employees the tools to do so.

## 14. Encourage Employees to Use An Organizer

There are dozens of organizing and planning systems. Whether employees use a paper system or a computerized system, it really doesn't matter as long as they have a system that works. Encourage employees to use their system to identify goals and activities, set priorities, record important dates, addresses, telephone numbers and other important information.

## 15. Encourage Employees to Tame Telephone Time

Encourage employees to manage their telephone time better by: limiting the amount of personal calls that they receive and make. Using e-mail instead of making calls and asking them to let the people who call them the most know the best times to reach them in the office. These simple steps will help to tame telephone time.

## 16. Stress the Importance of Being On Time

When people are late for meetings and for work, it wastes time. Talk to your employees about estimating their time needs and giving themselves enough time to arrive on time, start on time and finish on time.

## 17. Encourage Employees to Use Time Logs

Most people really don't know where all the time goes. This is why a time log can help. By recording your time in thirty-minute to one-hour blocks, you'll be able to see how and where you spend your time. You'll also be better able to identify and eliminate self-imposed time wasters.

## 18. Encourage Employees to Stand Up to Minimize Interruptions

Most people sit when they talk to someone, but if your employees stand up as soon as someone drops by, it sends the message that their time is limited. The other person will probably get to the point a little quicker and your employee can get back to work.

## 19. Encourage Employees to Get to the Point Quickly

Getting to the point quickly is a valuable skill. Encourage employees to identify what they want and need before they begin the conversation, and to think about the best way to say what they have to say.

## 20. Encourage Employees to Speak Up and Say No

Speaking up and saying no to things that you simply cannot or will not do, are two of the most effective time management strategies. Saying no and asking for help can be difficult, especially when it comes to people you want to please. But when employees do not speak up they fall prey to the stress and burn out associated with trying to do too much for too many people. Encourage employees to honestly evaluate their workload and say no when they simply cannot do anymore.

## 21. Encourage Employees to Balance Work and Personal Time

We cannot give to others, unless we first give to ourselves. Encourage employees to balance work and personal time. Encourage them to take vacations, recognize their stress systems and spend time doing the things that they enjoy. When employees have balanced lives, they are more productive at work.

## 22. Don't Try to Dress Up Boring Tasks As Fun or Exciting

Some tasks no matter how much you dress them up are simply dreadful. Don't insult your employees' intelligence by trying to dress up boring tasks as fun or exciting. Instead help them come up with an adequate system for going a good job and getting the job done on time.

## 23. Help Your Employees Learn to Manage Projects In Bite-Sized Chunks

Rather than allowing employees to become overwhelmed by the enormity of a task, help them to manage it into bite-sized chunks. Let employees set a date to start the research, begin the writing and complete the task.

## 24. If An Employee Seems To Have Difficulty Managing His Workload, Find Out What's Really Going On

You will have some employees who will not stay on top of their workload no matter how much guidance you give them. When this happens, try to find out what's really going on. Does the employee possess the skills and attitude to do the job? Is the employee simply unwilling to do the work? Are you placing unreasonable or unfair demands on the employee? Asking the right questions enables you to address the right problems.

## 25. Encourage Employees to Put Their Best Effort Forward

One of the biggest time wasters is having to do a job over that was poorly done in the first place. Encourage employees to give their best effort. It's better to take the time to do a job well, than to have to spend more time doing a job over.

# CONDUCTING PERFORMANCE APPRAISALS

The purpose of a performance appraisal is to assess an employee's work performance. An employee's work performance is not limited to how accurately he/she carries out his/her job function, it also includes: time and attendance, attitude, ability to get along with others, appropriate work attire, ability to follow-thru on assignments as well as the willingness to take the initiative.

A performance appraisal should be a joint venture with you and your employees taking mutual responsibility for what will be done to improve work performance. Since a performance appraisal is a joint venture, there should be no surprises on it. As a manager, it is your responsibility to consistently and continually provide your employees with verbal and written feedback so that your employees always know how they are doing. Think of the written performance appraisal as a culmination of the feedback you've been providing throughout the past six months or year.

Why are performance appraisals necessary? They are necessary because, the organization's objectives are achieved through individual performance. Performance appraisals enable the manager and worker to assess how well the employee is using his/her individual skills, strengths and talents to contribute to the organization's objectives. The performance appraisal also provides the manager and the employee with a formalized opportunity to discuss progress, goals and problem areas. Following are nine guidelines for conducting performance appraisals.

## 1. Prepare In Advance

Thoroughly prepare for the performance appraisal in advance. Jot down key points that you want to discuss, your observations of past performance, plans and goals for the future. Think about what you are going to say and how to best say it.

## 2. Let Employees Conduct A Self-Evaluation

Provide employees with blank evaluation forms and ask them to evaluate themselves. When they are finished, share your responses. Ask them to reflect on their past performance, goals, achievements and areas for improvement. This enables employees to take ownership of the evaluation process. It also gives you a sense of what your employees believe to be their strengths, achievements and weaknesses.

## 3. Start the Performance Appraisal Meeting by Stating Its Purpose

Let your employees know that the purpose of the performance appraisal meeting is to assess their performance, discuss plans and goals for the future and come up with an action plan for achieving performance goals. Let employees know that this is a joint venture and you will be discussing and comparing your responses to the evaluation form. Allow ample time for the evaluation, especially if problem areas are going to be addressed. Do not schedule the evaluation on a Friday. It only heightens the anxiety and it can spoil an employee's weekend, if the employee perceives it as unfavorable.

## 4. Know the Previous Goals and Any Mutual Agreements

When conducting the evaluation, it's a good idea to have a clear understanding of the previous goals and the mutual agreements to meet these goals. This enables you to measure an employee's progress against the stated goals and agreement. It also enables you to see if problem areas were addressed in the past. Further, it provides you with important information about an employee's accomplishments and past achievements.

## 5. Review the Employee's Job Description

Reviewing an employee's written job description provides you with important information about an employees' job function, role, responsibilities and the objectives for the position. Every employee should receive a written job description as soon as he is hired that outlines his duties, roles and responsibilities. The job description provides both you and your employee with a starting point for conducting the evaluation.

## 6. Make the Performance Appraisal A Joint Venture

Review and discuss the employee's job performance in detail. Let the employee know what you believe her strengths and areas for growth are. Find out what she believes are her strengths and areas for growth. Discuss how she's contributed to the department or organization and let her know what you'd like to see more of. Find out her ideas about ways to enhance her performance as well as the department. Find out what she needs to do her job better. Does she need training? Coaching? Mentoring? More flexibility? More room for creativity? Closer supervision?

## 7. Find Out About the Employee's Goals and Career Aspirations

Give employees an opportunity to talk about their goals and career aspirations. Find out where your employees see themselves in two years? Five years? Perhaps you might have some employees who want to go back to school. Or maybe you have employees who have skills and strengths that haven't been utilized yet. You may also have some employees who are interested in pursuing a supervisory or management position. Finding out about your employees' goals and career aspirations enables you to better support them in achieving their goals.

## 8. Develop A Plan of Action

Both you and your employee need to work together to come up with a plan of action for improving performance, strengthening skills, learning new skills and setting future goals.

## 9. Summarize Key Points and Try to End On a Positive Note

Conclude the performance appraisal meeting by summarizing key points and ending on a positive note. Provide a copy of the performance appraisal to the employee and ask the employee if there are any other questions or comments that he/she would like to make.

While it's important that you conduct fair and timely performance appraisals for your employees, it is also important that you provide opportunities for your employees to evaluate you. Most managers fail to do this, because they believe that their employees will use the manager's performance appraisal as an opportunity to grind an axe. Or they're not secure enough in their capabilities as a manager to solicit feedback about their performance from their staff. But in order to find out how well you're doing as a manager, you need to hear about your strengths and weaknesses from the people who not only work over you, but those who work under you as well.

The best way to seek evaluative feedback from employees, is to have them fill out an anonymous questionnaire. This increases the likelihood that they'll be completely honest and it removes the fear of reprisal. Once they complete the questionnaire, ask one person to collect them, place them in a sealed envelope and leave them in your mailbox. Some questions that you might want to ask on your manager's performance questionnaire are:

1. What would you say are my strengths as a manager?

2. What do you believe are my weaknesses as a manager?

3. What frustrates you most about working under my supervision and leadership?

4. On a scale of 1 to 10 with 1 being the lowest and 10 being the highest, how would you rate my communication skills? Team building skills? Please explain in detail.

5. What skills have you strengthened or ideas have you learned since working under my supervision?

6. How would you describe my management style? Please explain in detail

7. What do you want and need from me as your manager? Pleas be as specific as possible?

8. If you were the manager what would you do differently?

## *62 WAYS TO REWARD EMPLOYEES*

Everyone wants to be appreciated. Rewarding employees for their hard work is an important aspect of management. Recognition for a job well done almost always leads to another job well done. Yet many managers do not acknowledge their employees' good work or reward them for a job well done. Some say that they're too busy, while others simply don't care. But as a manager who wants to continually bring out the best in your employees, you can't afford not to make positive reinforcement part of your management tool kit. Here are 62 ways that you can reward your employees for their hard work.

1. Ask employees how they want to be perceived by the organization and have someone create a tagline on all memos and have business cards or desk calendars printed up with the tagline.

2. Create a special club for high performers and offer special perks like complimentary coffee or a gift certificate to their favorite grocer.

3. Allow more seasoned employees to act as mentors and informal supervisors and give then an extended break once a week as a reward.

4. Design your own thank-you cards and write a quote or two that captures the spirit of your gratitude.

5. Make a gift basket that contains things that the individual can use in his hobby.

6. Purchase three CD's by the individual's favorite artist.

7. Provide the individual or team with movie tickets.

8. Bring the person homemade lunch for a week.

9. Cover the person's desk with chocolate.

10. Bring the person fresh flowers or a plant.

11. Give the person half day off with pay.

12. Bake a batch of cookies and deliver it on a silver plated tray.

13. Let the person or team attend a training program of their choice.

14. Shine the person's shoes for a week.

15. Offer to dry clean two suits.

16. Bring in a massage therapist and provide your team with a 15-minute shoulder massage

17. Let the person attend a gala event at the organization's expense.

18. Serve them a champagne or sparkling cider brunch.

19. Provide toys or gifts for their children.

20. Let them choose their next assignment.

21. When an employee does an outstanding job, pay to have her car washed or wash it yourself.

22. Take the person to a matinee play or dance recital on company time.

23. If one of your employees does something that saves the organization money, make a formal presentation to your entire department and present the employee with a plaque or trophy.

24. Provide your team with a set of water goblets with: "We Succeed Everyday:" printed on them in gold foil ink.

25. Provide outstanding employees with certificates signed by the president that state their specific contributions.

26. Start a monthly president's luncheon and invite high performing employees to eat lunch with the president.

27. Leave colorful post-its with positive feedback on each employee's computer or desk.

28. Have an outstanding employee spend the day shadowing the president.

29. Ask the company president to send a thank you letter to an exceptional employee.

30. If an employee does something exceptional write a feature story on the employee and put it in the company newsletter. Or even better, submit it to your local newspaper.

31. Write a full-page acknowledgement letter thanking employees by name and place it in your annual report.

32. Create a "Good Effort" news release to recognize employees who put their best efforts forward even if it didn't lead to the results you wanted. Be sure to include what they learned from the experience.

33. Periodically give $5 bills or even $10 to employees or teams who produce excellent results.

34. Subsidize one week's subway or bus fare for an outstanding employee.

35. Provide outstanding employees with $10 phone cards.

36. Hold an auction for your team and let them bid on items such as: one evening of babysitting services, one week of free breakfast, coming in one hour late for two Friday's at the company's expense or pedicures at the local salon.

37. Pay an employee's traffic ticket

38. Offer to clean and organize an employee's office

39. Send the employee to a conference in another state.

40. Provide exceptional employees with a gold medal or ribbon pins that say "outstanding employee at XYZ company"

41. Create a monthly MVP card that allows employees to enjoy unusual company perks like: one-on-one time with the president, extended breaks, first dibs at office supplies.

42. Take photos of exceptional employees and create a wall collage that decorates your department wall.

43. Organize a staff retreat in the Bahamas. If you have a time share or summer home, host a staff retreat at your place.

44. If your team completes a project successfully, send a personalized thank you letter to the entire team outlining each member's specific contributions. Go one step further and have t-shirts or backpacks made.

45. Hold a raffle for members of an exceptional work group and raffle prizes such as: theatre tickets, a day of pampering at a spa or $50.

46. Pay membership dues for a professional organization.

47. Pay for a dance class, golf lessons, a pottery class.

48. Visit your local 99-cent store and create a personalized care package for employees.

49. Buy a journal or book of quotes for an exceptional employee.

50. Rent a movie and watch it on company time over popcorn and pizza

51. Provide outstanding employees with an engraved merit badge and a video with you making a thank you speech.

52. Take employees to a basketball, football or baseball game. Give them four tickets to a game.

53. If an employee must work late to complete a project give them carfare home or drive them home.

54. Arrange a whitewater rafting trip or a trip to a theme park.

55. Provide employees with tickets to a museum

56. Make a jazz, hip hop, country or classical music CD for an outstanding employee.

57. Host a theme party at the office complete with food and party hats.

58. Make a donation in the name of your team to the charity of their choice.

59. Give an employee the morning or afternoon off to volunteer for a cause they believe in.

60. Look through your videos, cassette tapes, CD's and books and create an antique/thrift care package.

61. Reward high-functioning, self-directive employees with more autonomy.

62. Recognizing your employees' efforts immediately and often. Give positive feedback. Whether you reward employees with kind words, certificates, plaques, meals, celebrations, seminars, additional perks and privileges or anything else that you can think of, it doesn't matter so much how you reward them as long as you reward them.

# 13 GUIDELINES FOR TAKING DISCIPLINARY ACTION

When disciplining employees you need to maintain your sense of objectivity. If you're too lenient, you run the risk of your employees taking advantage of you and continuing the detrimental behavior. If you're too harsh, you'll be perceived as cruel and unjust. And if you ignore problematic behavior, it will only get worse. So you have to find a middle ground. Following are 13 guidelines for taking disciplinary action.

## 1. Find Out How Similar Problems Have Been Handled Before

Before taking disciplinary action against an employee it's a good idea to do a little homework to find out how similar problems have been handled in the past by your organization. By finding out how such problems have been handled before, you can utilize a disciplinary method that is consistent with your organization's policies and culture.

## 2. Review Your Company's Policies and Procedures Manual

Go through your organization's policies and procedures manual to review what it says about handling absenteeism, conflicts between coworkers, substance abuse issues and other problems.

## 3. Keep Your Manager Abreast of What's Going On

Most bosses do not like surprises, especially problematic ones. Be sure to keep your boss apprised of any problems that he could find out about. By keeping your boss updated, you can draw from her experience to guide your decision in choosing the most appropriate course of action.

## 4. Prepare Thoroughly

Before you actually meet with the employee, review his file. The file should contain documentation of specific problems with dates, action steps and plans for follow-up. Use this time to collect whatever data you need to support your decision to take disciplinary action.

## 5. Explain the Purpose of the Meeting

Get to the point by explaining the purpose of the meeting. Find out why the behavior is occurring and determine what needs to happen for the behavior to stop. Don't make inappropriate assumptions particularly around the cause of the problem. Remember you're conducting a disciplinary meeting not a therapy session

## 6. Separate Cause From Effect

Focus on how the behavior is impacting on productivity, the work environment or the employee's work performance. While you want to find out why a behavior is occurring, you don't want to make this the focus of your meeting. You need to focus on how the behavior impacts the workplace.

## 7. Listen More Than You Speak

You need to listen to your employee to give him an opportunity to give you the full story and explain the reasons for his behavior. This will clear up any ambiguity and provide the employee with an opportunity to take ownership of the problem. Further, the more you talk the more you run the risk of saying something that will cut off any hopes of the employee hearing what you say as constructive and helpful.

## 8. Respect the Employee's Privacy

Meet in a private space and make sure that you're not disturbed. Don't discuss what occurred in the meeting with your staff or colleagues, it's none of their business.

## 9. Be Smart About Writing Employees Up

Whenever you write a disciplinary letter keep in mind that it becomes a permanent part of an employee's record that can leave a mark of lasting hostility. Before you write up an employee make sure that you've had some face-to-face meetings and despite your verbal warnings the employee shows no signs of trying to improve. Once you write up an employee, wait 24 hours before you send the letter. Review the employee's performance, how it impacts the workplace and what will happen if the behavior continues. If there are any phrases that are antagonistic or insulting rewrite the letter and focus on the core issues that need to be resolved.

## 10. Get the Employee to Walk In Your Shoes

Trade places with the employee by asking, "What would you do if you were the manager dealing with this kind of problem from one of your employees? This enables the employee to evaluate his actions and how those actions impact on his ability to perform his job effectively, get along with coworkers or contribute to your department in a relevant way. Sometimes you find that employees are harder on themselves than you would ever be.

## 11. Let Employees Select Their Own Disciplinary Tactic

I know this sounds crazy, but it really works. Here's how. When an employee's behavior is problematic and merits some form of formalized discipline, lay out two to three possible disciplinary action steps and let the employee choose the punishment that most fits the crime. For example, you might say, "In light of what you've done, I can suspend you for three days without pay, require you to develop a twenty page report focusing on the adverse effects of behavior such as yours or I can write you up send a copy to my boss and put you on a 30 day probation. This enables the employee to become an active participant in the disciplinary process and it allows him to reflect on what needs to happen to improve his work performance.

## 12. State the Consequences If the Problem Continues

Let the employee know what the consequences will be if he/she shows no signs of improvement or if the problem continues. Will you write the employee up? Suspend him without pay? Demote or transfer him? Or, will you terminate his employment. Make sure the employee is clear about what's at stake.

## 13. Summarize the Meeting and Set Up A Follow-Up Meeting

Conclude the meeting by summarizing goals, action steps and consequences. Establish a point of agreement in order to focus the employee's attention on improving work performance. Make it clear that you expect the employee to take the initiative in rectifying the situation. Set up a follow-up meeting to review the employee's progress.

# HOW TO FIRE EMPLOYEES ETHICALLY AND FAIRLY

One of the most difficult things that you'll ever have to do as a manager is fire an employee. There's no easy way around it, some employees will not work out no matter how much training you provide or how many warnings you give them. When this happens the smartest decision that you can make is to terminate their employment. But you must do so legally, ethically and fairly. Following are some guidelines to help you with the termination process.

### • Be Clear About Your Reasons For Firing

Be as clear in your reasons for firing an employee as you were in your reasons for hiring him. Has the employee consistently violated a company policy? Did he steal from the organization? Did she physically assault another employee? Did he/she sexually harass another employee? Be crystal clear about your reasons for firing an employee. Don't let it get personal.

### • Review Your Company's Termination Policy

Go through your company's policies and procedures manual and find out what the policy is for terminating an employee. By familiarizing yourself with your company's termination policy, you can use it to guide your actions.

### • Collect Your Data

Before terminating an employee collect all the data you'll need. Find out how much sick time, vacation time or personal leave the employee has accrued and follow your policies and procedures manual and your state laws on dealing with these issues once the employee is terminated. Put this information in the termination letter.

## • Make Termination A Last Resort

Make sure that you have given the employee ample opportunity to rectify the problem. If an employee has consistently not met performance standards and has not shown improvement despite warnings and opportunities to resolve the issue, then you probably have no alternative but to terminate his employment. If an employee does not demonstrate the skills to perform the job despite several meetings, trainings, coaching sessions and opportunities to grasp the skills required to carry out the job function accurately, then you probably have no alternative but to terminate her employment. Just make sure that you have done everything in your power to help the employee rectify the situation before terminating him.

## • Termination Should Never Be A Complete Surprise

Except in instances of workforce reduction or a serious violation of company policy, termination should never come as a complete surprise. You should be constantly meeting with problematic employees and clearly laying out expectations as well as consequences. Problematic employees should be made aware that if they don't attempt to improve their work performance termination is a possibility. Your supervisor should also be made aware that you are considering terminating an employee.

### • Try to Avoid Firing Employees On A Friday

If you can avoid it, don't fire employees on a Friday. Do it in the beginning of the week so that they have the rest of the week to look for a job.

### • Fire the Employee In Person

Never fire an employee by e-mail, voicemail or memo, it's cowardly and it conveys a lack of integrity on your part. Have a meeting and provide the individual with a termination letter. If the person refuses to accept it, have your human resources department mail it to him.

### • Meet the Employee On His Turf Or On Neutral Ground

Meet the employee in her office or reserve a conference room. This enables the employee to maintain some degree of control and it allows you to say what you need to say and exit. Further, if the employee breaks down, he can do so in the privacy of his office or the conference room.

### • Don't Argue

Don't argue with an employee about your decision to terminate. Explain your reasons. Get to the point quickly. Give the employee a few minutes to ask you any final questions and leave the office or conference room. If need be, discuss the status of any pending work, so that you'll be able to pick up where the employee left off. Give the employee the option to turn over unfinished work and keys to you or your secretary.

### • Manage the Employee's Departure

If things start to get ugly, you can have a security guard escort the employee to his desk and wait for him to pack up and leave.

### • Don't Talk About the Termination With Other Employees

If employees inquire about the staff member who was terminated, simply let them know that the employee is no longer working for the company and you are not at liberty to discuss the situation any further. It's about having the integrity to respect every employee's right to privacy no matter what the situation.

# SUMMARY POINTS FOR CHAPTER 5

- Every employee brings strengths and weaknesses to the job. Help employees to recognize their strengths and build on them. Help employees to recognize their weaknesses and take active measures to improve them

- Let your employees know what you want and need from them. Help them to stay focused on what's most important.

- Performance appraisals should be viewed as a joint venture with you and the employee working together to achieve the stated goals, set new ones and improve work performance.

- Make positive reinforcement part of your management tool kit by rewarding your employees regularly.

- When you have to take disciplinary action focus on behavior not personality.

- Make termination your last resort. And if you must do it, do it legally, fairly and ethically.

# 6

# *Getting In the Driver's Seat of Your Career*

What's the major difference between managers who advance quickly and managers who never seem to get ahead? In a nutshell: it's their ability to get in the driver's seat of their careers. When you have a burning desire to succeed, seek out opportunities to grow and map out a plan for advancing professionally, you'll move in the direction that you want to go. While complacent managers sit on the sidelines and complain about how difficult things are and avoid taking on new challenges, Smart Moves Managers are solution-oriented, focused and proactive.

A Smart Moves Manager takes charge of her career by developing a plan for learning, growing and advancing in her industry. She doesn't just wish for a more satisfying and successful career, she takes the initiative to make it happen. By doing so, she opens herself up to any and every opportunity that could potentially come her way. So use this chapter to generate ideas around how you can get in the driver's seat of your career and watch your career soar.

# 5 FUNDAMENTAL PRINCIPLES OF ACHIEVEMENT

In order to sit in the driver's seat of your career, there are five principles that you'll need to practice consistently. They are:

## 1. Develop A Clear Sense of Purpose

What do you really want to achieve, accomplish and contribute professionally? Why do you do what you do? Where do you see yourself in three years? Five years? Ten years? What do you really want to do, be and have? Having a clear sense of purpose enables you to focus your time, energy and resources on planning and pursuing your goals. This is essential for success.

## 2. Raise Your Standards

Any time you seriously want to change your life for the better, you have to raise your standards. You need to push harder, aim higher and stretch yourself further. Look at the different areas of your life and think about what needs to change in order for you to achieve an enhanced quality of life.

## 3. Change Self-Limiting Beliefs to Self-Affirming Beliefs

You must believe that you can achieve whatever you set your mind to, then you've got to act on your beliefs. Self-affirming beliefs provide you with a sense of certainty that enables you to pursue your goals persistently and diligently. So change all self-limiting beliefs to self-affirming ones.

## 4. Be Ready When Opportunity Comes Knocking

Sometimes opportunities look like problems. Sometimes they show up as situations that no one else wants to deal with. Being alert and open to opportunities creates greater avenues for you to do three things: increase your visibility, turn problem situations around and build your repertoire of skills.

## 5. Be Disciplined

Self-discipline is the channel through which all of your dreams are brought into fruition. Self-discipline enables you to put your feelings aside in order to do the work that is necessary for achieving your goals. Self-discipline allows you to control and direct your energy toward the accomplishment of your goals.

# *PROJECTING AN IMAGE THAT COMMUNICATES CONFIDENCE, COMPETENCE AND CREDIBILITY*

By now I'm sure you know that the manner in which we present ourselves greatly influences how others perceive and treat us. While no one wants to be thought of as boastful or egotistical, you certainly can't afford to shrink back into the shadows either. A Smart Moves Manager knows that in order to move forward professionally, he must begin by projecting an image that communicates confidence, competence and credibility. Here are some tips to help you.

- Think highly of yourself and the skills you bring to the marketplace. Believing in yourself is the first step in projecting a powerful professional image. It is essential to your success that your confidence comes through. Even if you are nervous or apprehensive, try not to let it show.

- Keep negative comments to yourself. Never badmouth a coworker, your boss or a former boss in public. You never know who's listening. Further, it makes you appear untrustworthy.

- Do an honest self-assessment. What areas of your personality, habits and work practices do you need to improve?

- Be reliable and be on time. When all else fails all you have is your word. Let your word be your bond.

- Project a positive attitude. How do you come across to others? What message are you sending through your behavior and body language? How do your bosses, employees and colleagues perceive you? Think positive, speak positive and be positive.

- Be cordial to everyone you meet from the CEO to the front desk receptionist. Even if you're having a bad day you must remember to be pleasant.

- Be easy-going. People prefer to work with people who are flexible and who don't make a big deal out of every little annoyance. By being easy-going, you'll come across to others as a team player and people will be naturally drawn to you.

- Handle proprietary information with care. Be the type of person who others can come to when they need guidance or a silent sounding board.

- Learn the technical skills and information required to carry out your job function successfully. Know how to do your job inside and out.

- Be an interesting person. People like and respect people who are interesting. Broaden your horizons and make learning a lifelong commitment. Cultivate your talents. Take up a hobby.

- Be an attentive listener. When people speak to you, try to focus your complete attention on what they are saying.

- Know how to read people. Reading people is about understanding that people have two faces: The one they present publicly and the private one. Reading people is about seeing beyond the public face in order to discern their true message and intent.

- Dress for success. Be sure to observe your company's dress code. Don't just dress for your position, dress for the position you want. Make sure that your clothes convey the image that you're trying to project.

- Adopt a role model. One of my role models is Oprah Winfrey. Although I've never met her, I admire and respect her a great deal. And the constant message that I get from watching her is, "use your life responsibly." I take this message to heart and use it as a catalyst to remind me that I am responsible for my life. Think about someone who you respect and admire and study his/her life. Adopt some of the principles that they live by and apply them to your life.

- Be the consummate professional. In all that you do, put your best foot forward. Be professional in your attitude, attire, behavior and your verbal and written communication. When attending company parties and events, watch your liquor consumption and behavior.

## INCREASING YOUR MARKETABILITY, VISIBILITY, AND INFLUENCE

Achieving your goals of increasing your marketability, visibility, and sphere of influence begins with three fundamental questions: How can you increase your skills, knowledge and resources? How can you bring additional value to your company? And how can you get others to recognize you and notice your ideas? Knowing what you have to offer and being skillful enough to promote your brand are key to increasing your marketability, visibility and influence. This section will show you how to do this.

Communicating confidently about what you have to offer is not an act of conceit, it's an honest expression of the faith that you have in your ideas, skills, expertise and talent. But showing the world how talented you are is not an easy task. Why? Because most of us are afraid to let our lights shine too brightly. We're worried about stepping on other people's toes, rubbing our colleagues the wrong way or shinning so brightly that it makes those who do not fully utilize their own gifts feel insecure.

To truly take charge of your career, you've got to let others know what you can do. You've got to seize every opportunity to hone your skills, promote your talents and contribute to the success of others.

## I. Increasing Your Marketability

The key to increasing your marketability is to figure out what you can do to bring additional value to your company. The more you bring to the table, the more you increase your value. What can you do to become more marketable within your organization? Do you need to get an advanced degree? Do you need additional training? Do you need to familiarize yourself with your industry's trade publications? Would it be a good idea to join a professional association? Can you think of some creative ways that you could increase productivity or save the organization a little money? Are there creative ways that you can generate additional income for your company? Can you develop a new program and get funding for it? Think of all the ways that you can bring additional value to your organization.

Every quarter you should conduct a self-assessment of your marketability and value in your current position. Some questions you should ask yourself are: What have I learned in my current position within the last three months and how am I using this information to improve my work performance and increase productivity? What are the required skills and expertise necessary for advancement? Do I posses them? What do I need to learn or strengthen within the next three months? Am I delivering more value to my organization and industry than I was six months ago? What is my evidence of this? What are my plans for continued growth? What do I need to do to build relationships with key people in my industry? Are there any trends or changes in my industry that I need to be aware of?

Taking time to assess your marketability, allows you to work on the skills and qualities that will enable you to move forward in your career. In addition to assessing your marketability, learn how to become an indispensable asset to your boss and your organization. Get a clear sense of what people in the top decision making positions want and need. Then, make it a habit of delivering what's needed.

If your job is at risk of being phased out, let your employer know that you are a highly competent and dedicated employee who would like to be considered for a position in another department.

Here are some additional suggestions for increasing your marketability.

- Think like an archeologist and dig for clues about ways that you can save time, money and build resources. Constantly be on the lookout for trends or changes in your industry and get on board.

- Think about the skills that will be necessary for the job you want three years from now and start developing those skills.

- Work with your supervisor to achieve your goals. Let your supervisor know that you'd like to be more of an asset to the organization and to her. Find out what needs to happen to make this a reality.

- Always stay in charge of the direction of your career. No matter what plans your supervisor has for you or what opportunities come your way, always remain in charge of your career. Be clear about what you want from your career and take the necessary steps to make it happen.

- Get out of your office. Attend trainings, industry meetings and talk to everyone. Find out what's going on in your industry and what you can do to contribute to the betterment of your industry.

## II. Increasing Your Visibility

In order to get others to recognize your true worth and pay attention to your ideas, you've got to increase your visibility. Everything you do, everything you say and everything you write provides you with an opportunity to increase your visibility. With careful preparation you can get key people in your industry to see you as a major player. Here's how:

- Build an impeccable reputation that gets your work noticed. Be known as an individual who always delivers high quality work on budget and on schedule. Project your most powerful image at work and let others see you for the virtually indispensable gem that you are.

- Get connected to highly visible people. Connecting with highly visible people allows you to attract the attention of those who can aid you in your career goals.

- Try to find out how others perceive you. Get a clear sense of what upper management, your employees and your board think about you. Be sure to present the kind of image that will keep you in the inner circle of your organization and get you invited to key events.

- Get involved in professional associations. Don't just join an association, volunteer to spearhead a high profile committee or special project. Many professional associations sponsor conferences and conventions where you can present a workshop or sit on a panel. This promotes positive visibility.

- Write articles for your industry's publications. If you've come up with useful strategies or helpful suggestions that will add value to your industry, submit an article to a professional journal or your company's newsletter.

- Design and conduct a training workshop on a subject that you're experienced in or passionate about.

- Look for ways to improve the status quo and present your ideas at the next manager's or board meeting.

- Volunteer to plan and organize a company party, picnic or fundraiser.

- Mentor another manager.

- Develop an agency wide in-house training program for new hires.

- Develop fun and innovative icebreakers for your manager's meetings.

- Support your colleagues in their efforts. You can enhance your reputation and increase your visibility by being seen not only as a team player within your department, but as a team player within your entire organization.

- Offer to run a meeting for your boss or give an informational presentation. This takes confidence and planning, but the results are worth it. Sometimes a great five-minute presentation can do more to increase your visibility than your years of experience as a manager.

- Put your talents and hobbies to good use. If you can sing, sing at your organization's holiday party. If you have a flair for decorating, assemble a team and decorate your department or the employee lounge. Let people see all of the gifts you have to offer.

## III. Increasing Your Influence

In order to increase your sphere of influence, you need to think about what you can do to make a more favorable impact on your colleagues, your boss and the overall organization.

Here are some questions for you to consider. What issues are most important to your supervisor? What issues are important to your board? Can you take on one of these issues? Is there a major problem that your organization is dealing with? Can you offer a solution? What type of products or services do your clients need? Can you come up with a plan to address these needs?

Following are some additional ways to increase your influence.

- Build relationships with influential people. Study their habits. Study how they communicate with people, how they carry themselves, who they associate with and how they handle pressure.

- Invest in your personal and professional growth. Attend training seminars and workshops. Invest in professional development books and audio and video learning programs. Read articles targeted to your industry. The more you know, the more you can share your knowledge with others. The more you share your knowledge the more you increase your sphere of influence.

- Build your reputation through word of mouth. Take a colleague to breakfast or lunch and swap ideas. Talk about ways that you can boost morale, increase productivity and contribute to your organization in new and exciting ways.

- Position yourself as an information guru. When you come across articles or books that you think a colleague or a manager may benefit from, pass them on.

## *MASTERING THE ART OF NETWORKING*

Effective networking enables you to develop contacts with people who: share similar interests, can help you get closer to your goals or refer you to people and resources that can help you. Here are eight tips that will help you master the art of networking.

**1. Talk to Everyone You Meet.** Talk to everyone you meet in professional settings, your place of worship, social functions, on airplanes, on the bus or train and even while you're waiting in line. You never know who you might meet. While you don't want to come across as pushy, there's nothing wrong with striking up casual conversations with a variety of people.

**2. Show Genuine Interest In Others.** Really make an effort to find out about other people's interests, hobbies, career aspirations and talents. If you have a contact or resource that could be of help, let the person know about it.

**3. Develop A Thirty-Second Commercial.** Be prepared with a short, simple explanation that sums up who you are and what you do. The general idea is to peak the other person's interest, not overwhelm or bore them. Use laymen's terms to explain what you do. Keep it short, precise and simple.

**4. Go Through Your Contact List.** Go through your contact list and write a few words about each person like: where you met them, what they do, how they can help you and how you can help them.

**5. Connect With People You Admire.** A wonderful way for you to develop lasting and mutually beneficial relationships is to connect with people who you respect and admire. People love to talk about themselves. And most people are willing to informally mentor someone who displays a genuine interest in their work.

**6. Talk to People Who Are Standing Alone.** Usually people who attend events by themselves welcome friendly and interesting conversation. Often people standing alone want to talk to someone, but they're too shy to initiate a conversation. Why not get the ball rolling?

**7. Don't Be Afraid to Approach A Group.** Although it may seem awkward at first, don't limit your networking opportunities by failing to approach people in groups. You can simply walk up to a group and say, "Hi, I don't know anyone here. May I meet all of you?" Most people will ask you to join their group or introduce you to someone else who is attending the event alone.

**8. Follow-up and Stay In Touch.** Meeting someone once is not enough. You need to follow-up with a phone call, note or e-mail and schedule a face-to-face meeting. Networking is only effective if you stay in touch.

# PLANNING FOR ADVANCEMENT

Far too many people mistakenly believe that if they do a good job, then those who are in key decision-making positions will recognize their true worth and automatically promote them. While it may work out this way for some people, for the majority it does not happen this way. If you want to move forward professionally, you need to develop a plan to make it happen. Here are some tips to help you:

• Identify the most important attributes that you need to advance to the next two levels. Don't just develop the skills and traits to land your supervisor's job, think about what you need to do to become your supervisor's supervisor. Figure out where you measure up and develop a game plan to close the gap between where you are right now and where you want to be in two to five years.

• Gain a better understanding of what your CEO and board look for in senior management and executive level staff and become the kind of person that they are looking for.

• Gain a better understanding of your immediate and ultimate career goals and develop an action plan of the next three steps that you'll need to take to move closer to your goals.

• Cultivate more effective and mutually beneficial relationships. Think about where you want to go and build strategic alliances with people who can help you get there.

• Seek out evaluations from your supervisor, mentor or a professional coach and ask them to identify: your strengths, areas for growth, skills you need to learn and experiences that you need to seek out in order to move closer to your goals.

- Be an original, but make sure you also know how to blend with your organization's mainstream and most visible group.

- Volunteer for assignments that provide high visibility and additional responsibility.

- Constantly look for ways to challenge yourself. Seek out new opportunities and challenges to help you hone your skills.

- Keep a log of the various ways that you've added value to the organization. If you can track how your efforts and ideas have led to increased productivity and revenue or reduced costs, you are showing your boss that you are an asset to the organization.

- Become familiar and conversant in the subjects that are of the utmost importance to manager's two levels higher than you.

- Turn you car or subway ride into a mini learning center by listening to professional development and personal enrichment audio programs.

- Delegate as much as you can so that you can focus your attention on grooming yourself to become a more valuable manager.

- Don't wait for your supervisor to send you to a training program. Take the initiative and seek out training programs that peak your interest and are relevant to your job function.

- Meet with a top manager in your organization and volunteer to do an assignment for him that does not conflict with your current job function or your supervisor's objectives for you.

- Seek out a mentor. Find someone who is further along in her career and schedule regular meetings about once a month to discuss questions, concerns and strategic career moves.

- Take responsibility for your career. Don't leave your career in someone else's hands. It's your career; take charge of it.

## SUMMARY POINTS FOR CHAPTER 6

- Develop a plan for advancing in your career.

- Apply the fundamental principles of achievement to your life and your career and you will achieve your desired results.

- Make continual learning a priority, do the kind of work that gets you noticed and seek out greater opportunities to influence others.

- To network for maximum impact, talk to everyone you meet and show genuine interest in others.

- Don't leave your career in someone else's hands. Take charge of it.

# 7

## *Success Beyond The Office*

A satisfying and successful career starts with a happy, healthy and satisfied you. The first law of success is, take good care of yourself. Strive to create a balanced life by taking time to do the things that give you meaning and that fuel you.

In my seminars and workshops, I often hear people say that they feel as though something is missing from their lives. Usually the thing that is missing is the sense of fulfillment that comes with living a balanced and authentic life.

We live in a world that constantly pushes us to move faster, disconnect from one another and look outside ourselves for the things that bring us happiness and joy. Between our careers, the demands of our families and life's responsibilities, it can be difficult to carve out the time needed to care for ourselves. But the thing to keep in mind is if you do not take good care of you, nobody else will. This is why it is critical that you make a conscious effort to stay balanced and put yourself at the top of your to-do-list. This chapter will focus on simple things that you can do to achieve success beyond the office.

# BALANCING WORK AND PERSONAL LIFE

When was the last time you stopped to think about where your time is being spent and how you feel about it? How many hours do you spend working on work related projects, thinking about work and planning your work? Well, all work and no play makes for a dull and stressed out manager. Work is important, but so is cultivating your outside interests and spending time with loved ones. Here are a few things that you can do to make sure that your work life doesn't overwhelm your personal life.

- Realize that you are in control of your life and your time is in limited supply. You have control over what you say yes to and what you say no to. Some choices are more difficult than others, like saying no to a parent's or child's request or establishing boundaries with your boss. But the reality is, you do have choices.

- Create a top priority list that outlines the things that are a priority for you at this time in your life. Having this list readily available will enable you to focus on what's most important to you when your life gets out of balance. Further, when you are clear about your priorities, you'll be able to spend more time doing what matters most to you.

- Learn how to say no. When friends, family, and people at work ask you to do things that you don't want to do or that don't fit within your schedule say no and stand by your decision. Of course this does not mean that you should say no to things that fall within your job description, but if you feel overwhelmed by your workload let your boss know that you cannot take on another project at this time unless he is going to provide you with additional help.

- Ask for help. Don't allow yourself to become overwhelmed by your workload or household responsibilities. Seek help. Ask your boss to get someone to assist you if you're working on a time consuming task. Ask your spouse, partner or children to pitch in and share the household responsibilities with you.

- Resign from any committees or organizations that drain you.

- Ask yourself: "What needs my attention at this time?" "What am I holding on to that I need to let go of at this time in my life?"

- Identify the things that drain your energy, no longer hold your interest or that make your life more difficult than it has to be. Look at simple ways that you could remove or handle the energy drains in your life.

- Schedule some down time. Everyday schedule some time to de-stress and unwind. It's important to schedule uninterrupted down time each day where you do something to relax your mind and replenish your spirit.

- Get regular check-ups. This is important. See your doctor regularly to make sure that you're in good health.

- Incorporate some form of exercise into your daily regimen. Physical activity reduces the adverse effects of stress and it energizes you for the day.

- Make time for friends and family. Spending quality time with friends and family is good for the soul and it deepens your connection to the people you care about. Sometimes we can get so consumed by work and life's responsibilities that we forget about what's most important. And when we come to the end of our lives, we probably won't regret that we didn't work enough, we'll regret that we didn't spend enough quality time with the ones we love.

## MANAGING STRESS

Stress is a normal part of life. It's inevitable. As long as we are living in a world that pushes us to catch up, keep up, stay ahead and get more done in less time, we will be faced with stress. As long as you're dealing with people who think and act differently than you, you will be faced with conflict, which almost always leads to stress. While you may not be able to eliminate all of the stressors in your life, you can certainly learn how to manage them. Here's how:

- Pay attention to your body. Your body never lies to you. It will tell you when you're tired, overwhelmed and under the weather. Pay attention to how your body responds to stressful situations. Do your muscles tense up? Do you get nausea or headaches? Your body will tell you when you need to slow down.

- Identify your stress symptoms. Everyone has their own unique response to stress. Some people respond physically. Some respond behaviorally. Others respond emotionally. Get a sense of how you normally react to stressful situations, so that you'll be able to quickly identify when you're undergoing stress.

- Try to link the stress to its specific source. Is the source of stress a person, a situation, a decision you've been putting off? If you know where the problem is coming from, you'll be better able to develop the most appropriate strategy for handling it.

- Get more rest. Not getting enough rest not only makes you tire out more easily, it also prevents you from doing your best work.

- Take strategic pauses and energy breaks. Relax your breathing and pause to get your bearings. Make sure you're on the right course and if you have gotten off course regroup and rechart.

- Watch your diet. When you're operating on overload there's a tendency to eat junk food or skip meals all together. Eat a balanced diet. Think of food as your fuel for the day. If you're operating on empty, how can you perform at your full potential?

- Slow down. Walk slower. Talk slower. Eat a leisurely meal and allow yourself to savor the flavor of the foods you eat. Get out of the office. Go for a walk. Go to a nearby park. Go see a movie. Go for a drive. Put an "out to lunch" sign on your door and take a nap.

- Adjust your schedule. Come in earlier and leave earlier. Or come in later and leave later.

- Take all of your vacation, personal, and sick time. You work for it. It's your right. You need time away from the office to recharge and refocus.

- Speak up to relieve stressful emotions. Don't keep your feelings bottled up inside.

# CREATING MORE JOY AND ABUNDANCE

Creating more joy and abundance in your life starts by recognizing that you have the power to live the life you want. If you adopt this attitude, you'll be able to create the necessary changes to live more joyfully and abundantly. Far too often we get so caught up in the business of life, that we forget to enjoy life's simple pleasures. It's easy to understand why. The demands of work and family, the high cost of living and our tightly cramped schedules make it seem like living a full and joyful life is an impossible dream. But you cannot allow life's pressures or your priorities to limit your quality of life. Even the smallest change can produce monumental results. Here are some suggested steps for creating more joy and abundance in your life.

## 1. Start the Day off Reverently

Starting the day off reverently is about being reflective, contemplative and appreciative. Whether you pray, mediate, quietly reflect, read something inspirational or write in a journal, starting the day off reverently enables you to get more in tune with yourself so you can focus on bringing more harmony into your life. You'd be surprised what starting the day off sacredly can do for you. It brings clarity, peace, comfort, inspiration and motivation.

## 2. Identify Your Most Compelling Life Interests

The simplest way to find your passion is to notice where it's hiding in the midst of your busy life. What do you find yourself doing in your spare time? What little extras do you do at work even though it's not part of your job function? What do you find yourself doing around the house that brings you joy? With friends and family? What did you do for fun as a child? What would you do if you were ten times bolder? What have you done in the past that surprised you with its' creativity and boldness?

## 3. Look for Clues, In Your Own Backyard

Examine your home and notice how you feel when you walk around. What room do you spend the most time in? What room do you feel most creative and relaxed in? Take out a journal and write down how you feel in each room. If there are spaces that make you feel drained or frazzled, think about small changes that you can implement to make your living space reflect your personality and passion.

## 4. Create A Sacred Space

Everyone should have their own sacred space where they can reconnect with themselves and let their creative juices flow. It can be a room in your home, a corner of a room or a special place that you go to escape, replenish and unwind. It can be a park, garden, beach, museum, bookstore, café, or any other place that feels special and sacred to you.

## 5. Honor Your Inner Promises

Most of us are good at keeping the promises that we make to other people. But, how many of us honor the promises that we make to ourselves? The reason we don't honor our inner promises is most of us secretly believe that the promises we make to ourselves are not as important as the promises we make to other people. Since there's no one to be accountable to but ourselves, it's easy to make excuses for not honoring our internal desires. What inner promises have you made to yourself? Did you promise to go back to school? Start an exercise regimen? Take up a new hobby? Spend more time with friends and family? Get that business you've been dreaming of off the ground? Take a much needed vacation? Fix up your home?

Our inner promises represent our hidden dreams and deepest longings. These are the things that create more joy and abundance in our lives. Let today be the day that you honor a long-overdue inner promise. After all, you only come through once.

## 6. Clear Away The Clutter

Let go of the things in your life that are no longer working for you and serving your highest good. Get organized. Don't be afraid to throw things away. You can donate them to a charitable organization. Believe it or not, clutter drains your energy. It also blocks you from receiving all the wonderful new things that await you.

## 7. Don't Let Adversity Defeat You

Adversity happens to everyone. We all are faced with set backs, challenges and situations that test our strength of will and resolve. But adversity does not have to define or defeat you if you make the decision to rise above it. No matter what you are going through or what you are being challenged with, know that no situation is bigger than you—your willpower, your courage and your spirit of perseverance.

Everything in life is a process, even adversity. If you don't go through the process, you will not be prepared for progress. You've probably been in a similar situation or known someone who has gone through what you are going through. Rely on what you know to be true to help you rise above an adverse situation. Honor what you know, do what you have to do to get through it and allow yourself to grow from the experience.

## 8. Build A Community of Support

In our society, there is a growing hunger for connection. With the advent of the information age, we've grown further apart as a community. E-mail and the internet have made it easier for us to be physically out of touch with one another. And with our busy schedules and commitments, we don't give the kind of care and attention that is necessary for deep, close-knit relationships. Relationships satisfy our needs for intimacy and connection. They nourish us and allow us to grow. At their best, they allow us to shed our daily burdens, face our fears, speak our truths and they provide us with the kind of support and caring that is necessary to live full and authentic lives.

To begin the process of building a community of support, answer these questions.

- Who are the people that you love and spend time with?

- How can you develop a deeper connection with them?

- Who can you share your secrets and insecurities with?

- Is there anything that is preventing you from having supportive relationships?

- What are you prepared to do about it?

- Who are the people that fall into your acquaintance category that you would like to develop deeper relationships with?

- Are there people at work who you consider friends?

- Are you missing close friendships in your life?

- What can you do to meet new people and rebuild old bonds?

- What will you do to expand your community of support?

## DEVELOPING A MILLION DOLLAR MINDSET

Can you afford to live the life you truly want? I'm not talking about being able to buy a Porsche, a million dollar home in a gated community or a vacation in the South of France. I'm merely asking whether or not you have the financial freedom to live out some of your hopes and dreams. If you're living in debt, it's hard to feel in control of your life. It's hard to finance your dreams or at least some of the items on your wish list, if you are barely making ends meet.

We live in a time of financial uncertainty and major layoffs, but that does not mean that you cannot take control of your financial life. In order to get financially fit, it's important that you get a clear picture of your financial habits. Following are some statements designed to get you thinking about your financial habits.

*I live within my means.*
*I do not make excessive purchases on my credit cards.*
*I feel financially secure.*
*I pay my credit cards in full.*
*I know where my money goes each day.*
*I have three to six months salary saved up in case of an emergency.*

*I am hoping that I will meet a wealthy partner who will help make things a little easier for me.*
*I always pay my bills on time.*
*I contribute to a retirement plan consistently.*
*I keep a log of my spending habits.*

Your responses to the statements should provide you with clearer information concerning your financial habits. If you are pleased with your responses, keep up the good work. If not, create a spending plan that allows you to live within your means. Here are some suggestions.

- Identify your income. Get a notebook and write down all of the money you take in like: a salary you receive from working, alimony, child support, and any other income that you receive on a regular basis.

- Know where your money goes. Write down all of your expenses like: your mortgage, rent, child support, household bills, car payments, loans that you are paying off and personal expenses like entertainment, hair and nail maintenance, clothing and other items that don't fall into your household category.

- Subtract your expenses from your income. If your income is greater than your expenses, look for more ways to save a greater portion of your income or invest more aggressively. If your expenses are greater than your income, look for simple ways to cut back on your expenses or create additional income.

- Pay off your debt. Whether it's a student loan, outstanding credit card bills, or a business loan, don't get trapped by overwhelming and outstanding bills. Get a copy of your credit report and repair it.

- Set a financial goal. Decide exactly how much you want to earn, save and invest each year. Then, break it down monthly. Let's break it down even further. How much money do you want to have at your disposal each week? Each day? How much do you want to have when you retire? Don't pull this number out of thin air. Really think about what you want out of life and how much money it will take to accommodate your desired lifestyle for the rest of your life.

- In addition to setting financial goals, set life goals that require large sums of money to achieve. Perhaps you want to buy a home. Take a vacation or two each year. Buy a car. Start a business. The important thing here is to estimate how much money you will need to achieve these goals so that you can start planning accordingly. Don't forget to write your goals down and set a deadline. The subconscious mind responds to dates and deadlines.

- Develop a goal attainment plan. After you have written down your financial goals and set deadlines, start researching the necessary steps you'll need to take to achieve your goals. Identify obstacles. Ask yourself: Why am I not at my financial goal already? What is going on inside of me and around me that's holding me back? What skills, information and resources do I need to acquire in order to achieve my financial goals? This is an important question, because in order to achieve a goal you've never achieved before, you have to apply a new skill, access a new resource or learn new information that you never knew or utilized before. Next, map out the key points of your plan and organize your steps by priority. Ask yourself: What is the first and most important step that I need to take to get closer to my financial goals? Then, take action. Do something every week to move closer to your financial goals. Read an article, attend a free seminar, surf the web, talk to people who have more income and assets than you and learn from them.

- Examine your attitudes about money. Examine your spending habits. Do you make purchases when you're stressed out or feeling low? Do you rationalize living beyond your means by saying: "I deserve this?" What thoughts and beliefs do you have about money? What have you discovered about yourself as it relates to your spending habits? What are you prepared to do about it?

- Respect your money. If you have allotted a certain amount of money for saving or investment use it for what it was intended for. When you tap into your reserves, you sabotage your financial future.

- Work smarter, not harder. Look for ways to create additional income without over exerting yourself. Seek out investment opportunities that will create passive income for you. Utilize your skills and talents in new and profit-making ways so that you can build up your financial nest egg.

- Start a retirement fund now. You won't be depriving yourself. You'll be ensuring a financially stable future. Contribute the maximum amount that you can afford.

- If you do not have a retirement plan at work, take a poll and find out how many other employees want one. More than likely most will say yes. Decide who will approach your boss to ask him or her about setting up a company retirement plan. Offer to do the research yourself.

- If your company won't offer a retirement plan or you're self-employed, open up an IRA (Individual Retirement Account). Go to your bank and ask about opening an IRA account there.

- Make the decision to become financially literate. Spend some time reading and learning about money. Read books like: "Rich Dad, Poor Dad," by Robert Kiyosaki, "The 9 Steps To financial Freedom," by Suzie Orman, and "Nice Girls Don't Get Rich," by Lois P. Frankel. Read the Wall Street Journal, Smart Money, Forbes and other magazines that focus on money.

- Attend financial investment seminars on a regular basis. Many banks offer free investment seminars for novices. Ask questions about managing money, creating wealth and planning for retirement. Talk to everyone at the seminar. Better yet, form a financial literacy group so that you can share ideas and resources about creating wealth and making smart money choices.

- Tune into television and radio programs that focus on money and business. Learn as much as you can from these shows. Call in or send an e-mail with your money management questions. It's your financial life. Take charge of it.

- Develop an attitude of gratitude. Start paying attention to areas where your life is already prosperous. Be thankful for what you have while creating avenues for more. Notice the many ways that you are blessed. When you develop an attitude of gratitude an internal shift in your consciousness occurs allowing you to reflect on the incredible abundance in your life.

- Give regularly to your place of worship or a cause that you believe in. Believe it or not, giving is what keeps the cycle of abundance and prosperity constant in your life. If you cannot give financially, consider the other ways that you can give back. There are a number of ways that you can give. The important thing is that you give.

## SUMMARY POINTS FOR CHAPTER 7

- Realize that you are in control of your life. Balance work and your personal life.

- Reduce your stress level by paying attention to your body and not allowing yourself to become overwhelmed by work or the pressures of life.

- Live life by your design, not by default. You have the right and the power to create more joy and abundance in your life. After all—you're worth it.

- Invite prosperity into your life by taking control of your finances, developing an attitude of gratitude and giving back.

# Conclusion

Congratulations! You have arrived at the conclusion of this book and now have the tools to excel as a Smart Moves Manager.

Let's do a quick review of what you've learned from this book. You now know how to:

- Lead and manage more effectively;

- Avoid the twelve fatal mistakes that managers make;

- Facilitate a team-centered work environment;

- Make office politics work to your advantage;

- Conduct performance appraisals and take appropriate disciplinary action when necessary;

- Boost employee morale and motivate your staff for maximum performance;

- Get in the driver's seat of your career and develop an action plan for advancement;

- Take the necessary steps to achieve success beyond the office.

It goes without saying that if you put the principles and strategies presented in this book into practice; you will reap the benefits of a rewarding and highly successful career. I thank you for choosing, *Smart Moves That Successful Managers Make* as your professional development resource and look forward to hearing from you soon.

Don't forget to visit me at: **www. strategiesforempoweredliving.com** and post a message for me on my blog to let me know how this book has helped you.

# Recommended Reading

Beth Jones, Laurie. Jesus CEO: Using Ancient Wisdom for Visionary Leadership New York: Hyperion, 1995

Beth Jones, Laurie. The Path: Creating Your Mission Statement for Work and for Life New York: Hyperion, 1995

Bixler, Susan Dugzn, Lisa. 5 Steps to Professional Presence: How to Project Confidence, Competence and Credibility At Work Avon, Mass: Adams Media Corp., 2001

Capezio, Peter. Powerful Planning Skills: Envisioning the Future and Making It Happen New Jersey: Career Press, 2000

Carusella, Marlene. Leadership Skills for Managers New York: McGraw—Hill, 2000

Ham, Alexander Motivating and Rewarding Employees: New and Better Ways to Inspire Your People. Hollbrok, Mass: Adams Media Corp., 1999

Hill, Napoleon. Keys to Success: The 17 Principles of Personal Achievement New York: Plume, 1994

Kimbro, Dennis. What Makes the Great Great: Strategies For Extraordinary Achievement New York: Doubleday, 1998

Nelson, Bob <u>1001 Ways to Take Initiative at Work</u> New York: Wordman Publishing, 1999

Payne, John & Payne Shirley. Management Basics: <u>The How to Guide for Managers</u> Avon, Mass: Adams Media Corp,. 1998

# *Other Books and Products By The Author*

## The Busy Woman's Little Book of Motivation.

This book will show you how to own your power, keep the cup full enough to feed yourself, get in the driver's seat of your career, break the habit of self-sabotage and take steps towards healthier relationships.

## The Single Mom's Little Book of Wisdom.

*The Single Mom's Little Moms Little Book of Wisdom* offers 42 insightful principles that will encourage any single mother to succeed, survive and stay strong.

## The Single Mom's Little Book of Wisdom Companion Workbook.

*This is the 8 ½ by 11companion workbook to* The Single Mom's Little Book of Wisdom. The companion workbook will show you how to move from principle to practice.

## Cool, Confident and Strong: 52 Power Moves for Girls.

This book provides pre-teen and teenage girls with the tools they need to take decisions that respect their values and boundaries.

## Young, Gifted and Doing It: 52 Power Moves for Teens.

From resisting peer pressure to setting goals and making education a top priority, this book is the definitive success guide for teens.

## Smart Moves That Successful Youth Workers Make.

In this book you'll learn: the 7 roles of the front-line youth worker, how to avoid the 10 biggest mistakes smart youth workers make and how to build assets in youth.

# Audio Programs

## 10 Foolish Mistakes Smart Single Moms Make

From using the children as pawns to trying to be all things to all people, this audio CD gives you the real deal on how to let go of the attitudes and behaviors that can sabotage your success as a parent and as a person on the path to excellence.

## What Smart Women Know: The 9 Essentials That Will Position You To Prosper

This audio CD offers 9 powerful principles that will position you to achieve lifelong success and abundant living.

To order any of these products go to:
**www.strategiesforempoweredliving.com.**

# Bring Cassandra Mack To Your Company or Organization

A successful organization with high performing employees begins with at the top. When supervisors and managers are equipped with leadership and management skills as well as practical tools that they can employ to motivate staff and address common workplace issues, everyone wins. The manager gets higher performing employees and the organization is better able to achieve its strategic objectives. Cassandra Mack's programs for managers can be conducted at your site as a full-day program or two half days. You decide.

## The Successful Manager: How To Lead and Manage With Vision and Victory

In this program you'll learn: the 7 habits of highly successful managers, the difference between management and leadership and how to wear both hats successfully, why you must have a manager's pledge, the 9 essential skills every successful manager possesses and how to contribute to a culture of leadership.

## How To Avoid The 12 Fatal Mistakes Managers Make That Lead To Lowered Morale and Decreased Productivity

In this program you'll learn how to: avoid the kinds of behavior and attitudes that can get in the way of your success as a manager, deal with problem employees and workplace negativity, the 13 guidelines for taking disciplinary action, how to fire employees ethically and fairly.

## Success Strategies for Women In Leadership

Whether you're a seasoned executive, a rising star in your agency, an aspiring entrepreneur or a young woman just starting to build your career, this seminar will show you how to make your strengths, talents and even your weaknesses work to your highest advantage. In this seminar you'll learn: the "real" differences between how men and women approach their careers and interact on the job and what we can learn from men, how to make career choices that protect your best interests and bring you the most value, tips for advancing in your career, how to handle personal attacks masked as "constructive" criticism or humor, how to avoid tears and what to do if you can't.

## Escaping The Superwoman Trap: Navigating The Tightrope Without Losing Yourself

You can tackle big problems with seemingless effort. Put out a crisis without batting an eyelash. Come in early, stay late and work through lunch without a single complaint. You can raise the children, support your partner and still find time to help other people put out the fires they create. Who are you? Super-woman—often to your own detriment. Nobody nurtures, supports and self-sacrifices better or more often than super women do. We do too much. Ask for too little and overextend ourselves to the point of crash and burn. In this program adapted from Cassandra Mack's book, *The Busy Woman's Little Book of Motivation,* Cassandra shares simple principles for overcoming the superwoman syndrome. You'll learn how to: keep the cup full enough to feed yourself, give yourself the best of what you've got, get over guilt and other ego trips, retrain family and friends to respect your time, energy constraints and priorities and slow down so that you can do the things that bring you joy.

# Listen to Cassandra Mack
## Live On the Radio

**Listen to Cassandra Mack live** on internet radio every Monday from 12noon to 1pm, eastern standard time as she tackles the everyday issues that impact us at work and at home. Cassandra's show **The No More Drama Hour of Power** provides insight for empowerment and tools for eliminating the drama that shows up in our lives as well as the drama that we bring upon ourselves. Addressing such issues like: dating, relationships, parenting, personal development, money management, living your dreams and getting ahead professionally, Cassandra serves up the issues straight with no chaser. Her guests range from industry experts to everyday people who have a compelling story to tell and insight to share.

To listen to the live broadcast go to Cassandra Mack's website: **www.strategiesforempoweredliving.com** and click on the radio show link.

# About the Author

Cassandra Mack is quickly becoming one of America's new leading voices on personal empowerment and excellence. As a nationally respected seminar leader, best-selling author and consultant who has worked with people from just about every facet of life, Cassandra offers success principles and strategies for empowered living that audience members can immediately apply at work and at home. From managers looking to raise the bar and bring out the best in their people to frontline employees looking to increase their value and productivity, to women seeking to sidestep unnecessary drama and bring their lives into sharper focus, Cassandra has literally helped thousands of people chart new courses for higher levels of personal and professional effectiveness and excellence.

Cassandra Mack, MSW is president and CEO of *Strategies for Empowered Living Inc.,* a New York based training and development company that offers keynotes, seminars and products in four areas: managing for peak performance, personal motivation, youth development and the empowerment of girls and women.

Cassandra has conducted keynotes, break-out sessions and business seminars for regional, state and national conferences and conventions. Some of the organizations she has worked with include: *Xerox, TIAA-Cref, Payne Webber, The National Mentoring Partnership, The Support Center for Nonprofit Man-*

*agement, Child Welfare League of America, Daniel Memorial Institute, National Resource Center for Youth Services, Big Brothers Big Sisters, Kean University, Urban Leadership Institute, New York University, Covenant House, Department of Education, Archdiocese Drug Abuse Prevention Program, Wildlife Conservation Society, Empire State Coalition of Youth and Family Services* and *the Civil Service Employees Association.*

She's written 7 best-selling books including *The Busy Woman's Little Book of Motivation.*

Cassandra is a contributing writer for *The New York Carib News, Proud Poppa* magazine and *The Harlem Parent.* She's been featured in *Black Enterprise* and *The Network Journal.* She's been a guest on *Good Day New York, What Women Want, Teen Talk* and numerous radio programs. Cassandra hosts a popular internet talk radio show under the New York Carib News entitled, *The No More Drama Hour of Power.*

To find out more about Cassandra's keynotes, products or talk radio show visit her company website: **www.strategiesforempoweredliving.com**

978-0-595-46371-8
0-595-46371-1

www.ingramcontent.com/pod-product-compliance
Lightning Source LLC
Chambersburg PA
CBHW070027210526
45170CB00012B/234